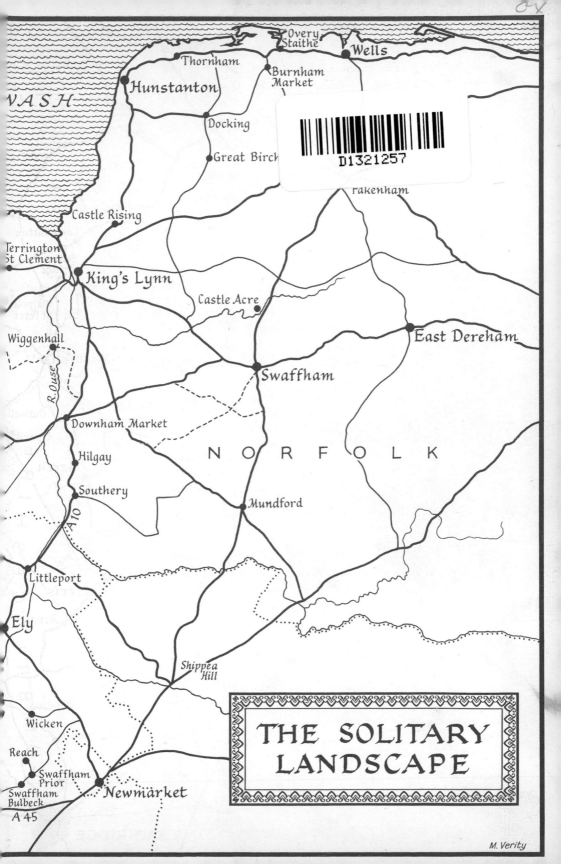

WASH

Overy
Staithe
Wells
Thornham
Burnham
Market
Hunstanton
Docking
Great Birch...
...akenham
Castle Rising
Terrington
St Clement
King's Lynn
Castle Acre
East Dereham
Wiggenhall
Swaffham
R. Ouse
Downham Market
N O R F O L K
Hilgay
A 10
Southery
Mundford
Littleport
Ely
Shippea
Hill

Wicken
Reach
Swaffham
Prior
Swaffham
Bulbeck
Newmarket
A 45

THE SOLITARY
LANDSCAPE

M. Verity

THE SOLITARY LANDSCAPE

THE SOLITARY LANDSCAPE

Edward Storey

with drawings by John Hutton

LONDON
VICTOR GOLLANCZ LTD
1975

ISBN 0 575 02052 0

Printed in Great Britain by
The Camelot Press Ltd, Southampton

for David and Karen—
who live where the fields were

ACKNOWLEDGMENTS

Even in a solitary landscape one is grateful for the company and conversation of friends and family, so I would particularly like to express my thanks to those people mentioned in this book who gave me help, information and encouragement:

Hugh and Renate Cave; Marian Edmunds; Jean Gill; Mrs F. Harris; Muriel and Neville Williams, and especially my parents whose talk of the fen-country and its people always keeps my interest alive.

I would also like to thank the Staff and pupils of Impington Village College, Cambridge, and David Kerrison, Producer of the BBC's Schools programme "Listening and Writing" for the opportunity of working together during several weeks when material for this book was being gathered.

For permission to use the quotations from the poems of Edwin Muir I would like to thank Faber and Faber Ltd, and my thanks are also due to Chatto and Windus Ltd for permission to use my own poem "Farm Hand" which first appeared in *A Man in Winter* published by them.

Other poems first appeared in *Critical Quarterly: Meridian* and *New Statesman*.

E. S.

CONTENTS

THE SOLITARY LANDSCAPE

PART ONE

THE BECKONING SUMMER

"I come out to these solitudes where the problem of existence is simplified. I get a mile or two from the town into the stillness and solitude of nature . . ."

Thoreau: Jan 7th 1857

Evening

I WOULD ALWAYS come back to this land for the low light of a late June evening, when the ripeness of wheat is seen before the grain begins to harden and the sun stays long on the low-tide of barley.

I never tire of its mystery and silence, never cease to be amazed at its expanse and history. Nothing hinders the almost horizontal rays of the sun as it moves very slowly towards the edge of the world. Its warmth deepens the colour of farm-buildings, the red-tiled roofs of barns and the russett bricks, the weathered feather-boarding of sheds and the machinery that now stands idle.

In the early part of summer especially there is always this feeling of waiting and expectancy at evening. The farm-workers have gone home, the travellers to work have sped back on their anxious journeys between business and the place where they sleep. Sheep graze more safely now than they could have done at eight o'clock this morning, or at five o'clock in the afternoon.

I am standing now on what is, for me, a familiar and favourite stretch of the fens, the north bank of the River Nene between Peterborough and Whittlesey. It has, in recent years, lost some of its appeal because the river-side road to the city (which was once a deserted road with a toll-gate at each end) has become a convenient and popular alternative route for work traffic.

But when it is quiet, as it is at this moment, it still offers a good beginning to a particular landscape—the solitary landscape of the fen country that spreads itself before you for as far as the eye can see.

The western horizon is broken by the shadowy outlines of the city, the tall blocks of flats and office-buildings competing with the silhouette of the cathedral. Northwards I look again over Prior's Fen towards Thorney. To the east the river takes its monotonous route to a muddy outfall in the Wash. Behind me are the local washlands of the south bank and the rows of willow trees that lead into the small fenland town where I was born.

Already the herons are beginning to take up their positions along the river-bank, as they do each evening; their long whitish necks jutting out like peeled sticks, their heavy grey bodies and big wings hidden by the tall riverside grass. They wait, and wait. Only their eyes move, unless some late passer-by disturbs them. They feel the fish swimming towards their

legs. They hypnotize them with their presence. Then they strike, catch
and swallow. And when the ripples melt into the bank they wait again,
hour after hour into the darkness—each kill, one fish less for the anglers of
Nottinghamshire and Yorkshire to pull out at the week-end.

I have watched the herons along this piece of river for many years.
Each year I choose one that I then believe to be the same one that I shall
always watch. He is the descendant, the successor, of the very first heron
I ever wrote about, the "clay-grey . . . scraggy heron" whose plumage
defied description until I saw him in relation to the landscape beyond the
river, a landscape of brickyard chimneys and clay-pits. That first old heron
was the colour of the ancient clay brought up from the pits we call 'knot-
holes'. Each year I try to find one that is just like him:

> Each night I come to find him here
> where mist has power to disguise
> the breadth of river and protect me
> from his cold and glassy eyes . . .

These fenland waterways are popular fishing-grounds for the northern
angling associations as well as for the heron and common gull. When the
fishing season begins scores of coaches arrive bringing hundreds of men
with their fishing rods, baskets, maggots and keep-nets to line the banks
and cast their hopeful hooks into the water. Some of the matches can earn
the lucky angler big money on a Saturday or Sunday afternoon. Some of
the catches bring envious fishermen from many miles away to compete.
Sometimes such an invasion can be irritating.

But there's not an angler in sight now. Only the herons wait. Only the
sheep munch in a cluster at the year's sweetest grass. And the swifts and
swallows flash and weave in a tangle of flight as they hunt the air for
insects and moths.

The light is still on the fields but it is deeper now and richer. An hour
ago it was shimmering and transparent, liquid and golden. As the wind
moved through the wheat you could see the light flow. Now it is beginning to set, beginning to seep into the dry stalks and the dark earth. There
are no clouds to be scorched and burnt by the huge sun. It is now a giant
poppy on the horizon; losing shape, fading slowly, shedding its limp, red
petals.

It is a quiet ending after so much promise. Distant church spires that
were prominent in the sun's light have disappeared. The farm-buildings
now blurred in mist are like pencil-sketches that have been half-erased

from the sky's page. I have stood on this piece of ground for so long that I feel I have taken root in the soil. I feel that when I want to move I shall not have the energy to pull my feet from the grassy bank. My roots go down as deep as the sky is high, as if I'm fixed here for ever between heaven and earth, between day and night. Again, I come for a reason. This, for me, is where all things start—every word, line and feeling.

Why, I sometimes wonder, won't the words come from the hills, or the sea, the dales or the woodlands? Why only here where the flat land is sometimes seen as nothing more than the floor of the sky's cage, where the horizon is so far away and so low that you can almost see the curve of the earth? Why, as a writer, do I always have to come back to this landscape when I want to write?

Certainly I believe that landscapes are important to a writer, whether he is a nature poet or a novelist, a prose writer or a dramatist. He takes from it his images, his scenes, even the speech-rhythms he uses. We are all products of some kind of landscape. Our geographical environment influences us as much as our social environment. Places have their own spirit and character. We take, absorb, interpret and we give back. Those who do not settle for long in one place, or feel that they don't belong anywhere, do not necessarily contradict this. For them there is always the search, the departing and arriving.

Many writers reveal their debt to a "particular landscape" in their work. The Brontë sisters would not have written the same novels had they lived in Cardiff or Southend. And it's not just simply a question of description. The Brontës did not only describe their landscape. They went beyond language and gave to the moors, to every grey house and stone wall a life and character that they had felt over and over again. They knew their landscape intimately. They felt it, breathed it and translated it as part of their own character and existence. It was part of them.

The same can be said of Thomas Hardy and Dorset, or of Wordsworth and the Lake District, or of Tennyson and the Lincolnshire Wolds, and certainly of John Clare and his Northamptonshire countryside. The sound of their speech, the rhythm of their voice, the identity of their imagination are all born of, and are part of, a particular landscape. Some, like wild-flowers, do not always transplant easily and grow much better in their native soil. Without them the earth would be poorer.

I tell myself this with some conviction, for I do not transplant very well either. For me the hills, mountains, lakes and woodlands of other counties have their beauty and their appeal, but they do not feed or satisfy the

heart's hunger in the same way that this corner of Cambridgeshire does.
I go to those landscapes when I need to rest. I come back here when I need
to work. What I am, what I have done, what I look for and what I feel, is
determined by these low fields, these farms, people, rivers and skies. They
may not appear very significant or spectacular to the outsider or the
passer-by, but they are mine. I never tire of them, for I have not even
measured the extent of their riches. They are there and their spirit is there.
I try to feel that spirit and relate it to what I put on the page.

Perhaps it is significant that these fields once belonged to water, either
flood-water or sea water. Often, on evenings such as this, you get the
feeling that they are trying to return, that some power is pulling them
back into the sea whilst some other power is trying to hold them back
from the water's edge. It is a silent conflict, just the feeling of two forces
pulling in opposite directions. I watch and try to understand their hours
of uncertainty. It is a loneliness at the edge of a place where neither sea nor
land will give in to each other and it is a time of day not always acceptable
to local people. The unreality, the eeriness, the overpowering presence of
the spirit of this place follow you around. In these moments of drifting
greyness and stillness we feel less secure, less in command of a landscape
that man has done so much to tame.

> You can't explain it, this
> mystery of air and water,
> low fields and distances.
>
> Somewhere behind the sky
> a weak sun spills its light,
> staining the silence.
>
> Bare trees on boundaries
> are half-erased; roads
> lose their identity.
>
> Men use what they can of the
> light's dying, ploughing
> from memory into the dark.
>
> An owl slips from a cloud,
> sweeping huge wings
> over its slaughterhouse.

The mist pushes horizons
out to sea, towards
some long-forgotten shore.

And all that's left is this
vague emptiness, or world
too strange to ever have a name.

Night

Behind me now the huge black shape of the river lock rises as sinister as
a guillotine. Lights have come on in The Dog-in-a-Doublet, an inn
that has been popular with anglers and wildfowlers for many generations.
Strange deeds and triumphs are still related there over a pint or two of beer
but the characters and the circumstances are very different from those of
years ago.

From its different windows you can see the sun rise and the sun set. In
winter you can watch ice-skating on the frozen fields opposite or in
summer see the harvest being gathered in only a few yards away. Opposite its front door you can still see the remains of the old bridge that used
to cross the Nene in coaching days and there are still the original stumps of
willow trees that once guided the traveller through the flooded washlands.

The fields have a deeper silence now. The individual crops of wheat and
sugar-beet, potatoes and barley, become as one, a thousand acres of roots
growing and of grain ripening. You cannot see or hear, but you can *feel*.
You are in an open boat at night on the sea, feeling the gentle rocking
motion of calm water. You surrender to the sensation. You become one
with the earth, air, water and sky. You become part of the night.

In the distance the tiny lights of the city perforate the horizon. The river
has the uneven shimmer of dull steel. The sheep now are only sounds on
the bank, snatchings of grass and shadows of cloud until the lights of a
passing car shine in their eyes and, for a moment, the grass is littered with
dazzling stars.

Some of the herons are still there, waiting, stalking, sometimes stabbing
the dark water. But one by one they rise from the water's edge like ghosts
in black and, with broad wings, fly back to their trees a mile away.

I go back to my parked car and decide to drive home. As soon as I
switch on my headlights and take the river road I am aware of the great

multitude of insects filling the night-air. The moths especially get drawn into the beams of the car lights and swirl like snowflakes towards me. It's not unlike driving through snow. The white, furry wings splash on to the windscreen and stick. For the restless swallows and swifts each passing car makes hunting easier. They swoop, dive, bank and rise with such speed in and out of the lights' beams that I am always amazed at their skill and timing. The split second accuracy that they need between each moth smacking on the grille of the car or being caught by the birds provides an astonishing act of aerial acrobatics. The birds appear to make no problem out of flying into the path of a car travelling at forty miles an hour and escaping safely with another morsel for supper only a hair's breadth later. They have perfected these crazy skills so well that you see few, if any, casualties on the road next morning, even though some cars travel considerably faster than forty miles an hour.

There are often casualties of another kind. Gulls do not always make it and, in the daytime, skylarks too become victims of motorists with not a minute to live. Sheep also suffer at the hands of reckless drivers who take the opportunity to tear along this narrow, unrestricted stretch of road at irresponsible speeds. For them the countryside is always an anonymous area of land between buildings, a no-man's-land that should be travelled through as quickly as possible, irrespective of the cost. So little time is saved in the end that I can never understand the rush.

I think I have learned now when to be on North Bank and when not. Friday and Saturday nights are no longer the right time, nor are the beginnings or ends of the working day. But tonight is a good time and now there's no need to even look at my watch. The world has quietened down and the earth gives a long sigh of relief.

I drive slowly, with the window down, listening to favourite night sounds, smelling the familiar night air. Somewhere out there might be the beginning of a new story, or a new poem, a new book or just a new sentence. It may come before sleep or wake me early in the morning. I journey in hope.

I look up. The sky is dark enough to let the summer stars shine, dark enough to make the yellow square of lights from distant farm-cottages look warm and inviting. The harsher lights of a town or city will come hard after such a night.

Morning

I would always want to come back to this land for the thrill of the day's beginning, the rapid spread of light over the sky and the quick brushing away of the baggy-eyed clouds.

I woke just before six o'clock this morning. The sparrows were already arguing noisily outside my window, their tuneless chirping chipping away with the monotony of a stone-mason's chisel. The silvery sky deepened to an intense blue. The sun, bright as a brassy cymbal, looked determined to stay with us until it had completed its journey towards the opposite horizon.

This is a land where, in summer, you can see the sun for fifteen hours as it curves over the arch of heaven from east to west. Only a few rooftops or a few trees break the perfection of its circle, only the clouds hide it from view.

Above the chatter of the sparrows I could hear another persistent tapping, a hollow, metallic sound that came down the chimney. I listened for several minutes trying to identify the sound that had the short staccato rhythm of morse code. It puzzled me. Was there some uninvited visitor nibbling away in the roof? Later, when I went out into the garden, I saw a thrush perched on the television aerial cleaning its beak, its honing movement as quick and casual as a butcher whetting his carving knife. It became a habit and for several mornings during the weeks that followed it was one of the first sounds of the day—that and the sparrows, and the swifts, and the clink of milk bottles from the early-rising milkman. Only rarely do I wake in time to hear the real dawn chorus. Usually I return from sleep only to be greeted by those more domestic sounds of songless birds, the eagerly awaited postman and the lazy paper-boy slamming the gate.

But what of today's morning? The sun's promise is being fulfilled. Already at nine o'clock the day is hot and cloudless. It's a day that will ripen the corn and make the waterside flowers blossom for their brief life, a day that must be lived out of doors where the fields beckon and new sensations await.

The first roads I take are busy with people still going to work or on holiday. The main road leads to Norfolk and the sea. It is also a major trunk road between the Midlands and the East coast ports, so it is an active road, a noisy thoroughfare that offers few pleasures to the sauntering motorist. But away from this constant coming and going there are roads that are usually empty, roads that stretch for miles and miles, straight and predictable. Roads that only go towards the distant horizon. Like our waterways they are a feature of the landscape.

Here there is always a long way to go.
The roads do not encourage you into
deceptive corners or an enticing ridge
as they do in hill-country. On this edge
of earth's platform they beckon beyond
a few trees or farmhouse, separating a land
that sulks below sea-level. Look any way
and these roads narrow towards the sky,
towards that space where the clouds grow.
You can take these roads at their face value,
they have nothing to hide and what you cannot see
is beyond the boundary of the naked eye.

You may feel that a man's stature should be measured
by his landscape, his bones hard, his fissured
brow a replica of the rock's forehead,
the contours' rhythm caught in his stride.
Not here. A man gauges his worth against
intemperate winds, feeling his face rinsed
by the rain flung in from the sea. He works
not by stone walls but by those open dykes
where rats nest in the soft peat and eels
slip through the dark stream like a vague thought.
You can hate these roads or find, like hills,
they lift you, step by step, out of the soul's drought.

The solitariness of this landscape is often intensified by the presence of a man in the picture. Even in close-up he looks so small against the immeasurable space around him. His presence gives perspective to the vast background. There are no hills for him, no mountains or stone walls. This land rises towards the sea. Travelling north-east, as straight as the wild goose flies, the first mountains you would have to cross would be the Urals of Russia. On a clear day the distance is infinite. You need a man in a field to help you measure how far you are looking. He is the needle by which you gauge the length of your eye's journey.

Most men who work in these fields now do so alone, or in pairs, often separated by an acre or more of the same crop. The days of gang-labour on the farms have largely disappeared. The machine has, thankfully, taken over much of the back-breaking work that years ago had to be done by hand, by women as well as men. Now, one man goes out with his machine, his tractor and harrow, his combine or beet-lifter, and the field is his, all day and every day until the work is complete. He can be like the sun, part of the landscape from first light until dark.

There is a man working now in a field where I saw him working yesterday. The nearest house is three miles away and the nearest town about six. He may not speak to another soul until he goes home at four o'clock, or six o'clock, or nine o'clock. He has been there alone, working on the land, looking after the crops, hour after hour. He has done it for years, season after season, one crop after another. He will have company perhaps at harvest time. Sometimes there may be someone else in a nearby field. He may go home for his tea and come back in the evening for another few hours. He takes the silence, the space, the sun, rain or relentless winds of winter for granted. He knows the sudden change to spring and the long days of summer. Today he does not look up at the lark singing above him. He only glances at me as I wave from the broken field-gate. More than many he can say when he finishes his day's work that the day has been his, whatever its worth. He may not have seen the wind hurry through grass or heard the familiar small-talk of birds in a hawthorn hedge. He has worked alone from morning till dark hoeing the long rows of sugar-beet, his arms making a pendulum for the sun's clock, his back an anvil for the afternoon's heat. His only companions have been the brief shadows of cloud passing over his land, or the occasional lark making sure that the earth was still there, watching over the solitary man who does not stop his labour to listen for a moment to such an outpouring of song.

I notice also today how much colour there is again on the grass verges and along the dykesides. Clusters of white mayweed, patches of moon-daisies, flowering thistles, cat's ears, ragwort, white campion, dandelions, mallow, poppies and buttercups—a dozen varieties of wildflowers that have not yet been extinguished by the machine or weed-killers, a tangle and ramble of grass and blossom that make me repeat again that exultant line of Gerard Manley Hopkins, "Long live the weeds and the wilderness yet".

On one side of a narrow dyke that divides two wheatfields the poppies are so numerous that they run like an open wound on the earth's flesh, a shock of red so brilliant and luminous that I stand amazed at such a spectacle. The white of the moon-daisies intensifies the vivid glare of the poppies. The burning yellow of the giant dandelions heightens the bright purple of the loose-strife.

I walk a hundred yards along the dykeside and count the variety of flowers. Hidden among the long grass and on the lower banks of the dyke I find a mass of mallow and toad-flax, bladder campion and bindweed, dead nettle and sorrel; fourteen different kinds of weeds in flower, and there just for the looking.

Several of the narrower dykes are choked now with reeds, bulrushes, sedge and other people's rubbish. The tall reed-mace are ripening, their long brown heads creating a fantasy of pantomime armoury, a strange army of make-believe soldiers who will never attack.

The abundance of colour on the grass verges and on the fields' headlands has kept my eyes from admiring the crops around me, but now I look at the wheat and the barley, the beet and potatoes, all coming to perfection, all hoping to avoid storms, blight and disease. The pale sage-green of the wheat crops of only a few weeks ago has already turned stone-coloured and dry. The barley is moving like wind-blown sand and the potato flowers settle like a swarm of butterflies on the cool dark leaves.

I watch three skylarks rise from the field and go high into the air above me. Their song is less urgent than it was earlier in the spring. They stay airborne for a while, trying the morning air, making sure that the sky is still there and the earth below. Then they parachute down again, one by one, to the potato field and disappear.

The other fields are empty and silent. I can see no one else working as I walk back to my car and drive out, deeper and farther into the waiting fens. But the atmosphere I have felt since leaving home an hour ago still remains, the sense of limitless space and uninterrupted skies, the earth flat enough to show church spires ten miles away, the roads going on and on, the distance always beckoning.

Isolated barns and white farm-houses hold these distances together and yet separate the day. Time does not seem to matter here. But where else is time more important? The season moves on, slowly, demandingly. The season dictates. It is fickle but inevitable. It plays, and it always wins.

Someone new to this land said to me the other day, "What puzzles me is the inactivity . . . you seldom see anyone doing anything . . . and yet the crops grow, the scene changes, the fields are cleared . . . who does it?"

Removed from winter the sky blossoms,
Trees hatch from their black shells,
fledgelings tremble like leaves trying to fly . . .

Things happen here in slow and subtle ways and you have to watch closely to see man and the seasons working, day after day, until the scenes change and the fields are cleared.

Afternoon

After lunch I go to see some friends who live in an old house on the edge of a farm. The house is square and solid, sheltered by trees planted by its builder two hundred years ago. Martins have built their own houses under the eaves, seven or eight nests that have (with many nests before) provided summer homes for these restless birds through several generations. They have come again to spin their halo of flight around this quiet house.

The room, with its high ceiling, stays restful and cool even on a warm summer's afternoon. The windows are open and I can smell the honeysuckle on the wall outside and the tobacco plants in the flower border. Beyond the window I can see the garden path curving towards a privet hedge and the gravelled drive that leads to a small bridge crossing a dyke.

I sit talking for some time with the owners of the house and we fail to notice that it has started to rain. I think it may have been the growing coolness from outside, or the stronger scent of the blossom, or the sweetness that comes to dusty leaves at the beginning of a shower, or perhaps it was just the afternoon's subtle stillness that made me look up, but when I did I was surprised to see the leaves and the nearby out-buildings wet.

So the weather changes our conversation and we talk about which crops could have done with the rain a month ago and which ones will benefit from it now. I am fascinated by the rain. It is gentle today. It falls so languidly we could be watching a film of rain in slow motion.

The ivy on a small bridge glistens. The leaves gather the rain and let it fall slowly in crystal drops. There is hardly any sound to the rain for it is absorbed quietly into the foliage and soft earth. The trees are still. In the rain they have been transformed, fixed, put into a deep sleep. Between those trees that are near to the house and the trees that are behind them the rain has drawn a fine curtain, a grey, transparent veil that has changed the colour of the distant foliage. Those leaves have taken on a blurred and mistier blue. There is no space now between the earth and the sky, between one branch and another, or between the bridge and the trees. It's as though the garden and the clouds have made their own marriage, with the rain as their blessing. The only movement that disturbs, but does not mar this stillness, comes from the martins. They fly round and round the house, tangling and then untangling their flight, weaving a pattern through the rain that is there for a moment and then gone and then brought back again. It hypnotizes. I watch them for several moments. They appear as aimless as moths searching for the brightness of a lamp. As soon as their flight-path looks established they veer away and return to their starting point.

The silence is broken, but not spoiled, by the room clock chiming quarter to four; three sequences of two notes, each sequence a falling cadence that thankfully leaves the hour untold, the day suspended in a moment that will never reach four o'clock. I feel that if Time has to stop then there could be no better moment for it to happen. But this is selfish, if not wishful, thinking. My feeling of total contentment, though, makes me decline the invitation to tea. I have to be home before evening and I leave before the hour is up and the clock chimes four.

About a hundred yards from the house I stop to give an old man a lift to the village. His coat smells of the rain and his tobacco. He tells me he has worked on the land for fifty years and has often worked all day in the rain until every stitch of clothing was wet through. I noticed he walked with a stoop, his back quite bent, his head low. Sitting beside me now he looks much older, his skin is tanned and cracked like old leather. His hands are rough and cramped with arthritis. He told me he had a daughter who lived near London. She wanted him to go and live with her now her own family had grown up.

'Don't you want to go?' I asked.

'I tried it for a week or two but I soon came back.'

'Why was that?'

'Too much noise and nothing to look at, only houses.'

He was silent for a moment and then said, 'Besides, you can't be what you're not, can you, and I don't intend to try.'

I dropped him at the village post office where he was going to fetch his pension. His eyes had the look of eyes that have been hurt by the thought of cities, or old age, or hopelessness. His only pleasure came from talking about the fields that had bent his back and deformed his hands.

> He has not felt the slow process of the wet earth
> gnawing his flesh. The black furrows have ingrained
> their map of soil into his hard skin, the reward
> of fifty years' work in the heart of the fens.

Summer may have ripened his arms to mahogany brown
or drenched birdsinging warmth on to his bent back.
But winters outlive summers by a long time
and now his bones ache with their lifetime of sweat.

No soap or scrubbing can remove those years.
Scarred, like a miner who has knocked at the black
walls of the earth's heart, he has his own wounds
to show, to lay bare on the table of old age.

Yet ask him to move from this mysterious land
and he will mock you with his far-fixed stare.
Those new-ploughed furrows glistening in the fields
warm the cracked hands, stir his low-burning fire.

Return

I drove home through Chatteris and along Forty Foot—one of those long
drains cut by Cornelius Vermuyden in the seventeenth century. It's not
a road that everyone likes. On one side there is a drop of several feet into
muddy water, on the other side there is an equal drop into the fields that
have slowly subsided over the years. It is like being on a tightrope. The
road stretches taut and narrow for five miles before you turn with relief
towards Pondersbridge. On a windy day you feel very exposed and precarious, the pressure of wind on the car makes it even more difficult to
keep a straight and steady track. In time you feel it is not the car that's
moving but the road, that narrow wire on which you are trying to keep
your balance. The only thing worse than a strong wind is the mist, for
then the road disappears and reappears with alarming unpredictability,
tempting you to drift to one side or the other. I know people who do not
even like that part of their journey when it is taken in broad daylight and
perfect conditions. My own two worst trips have been in thick November
fog and a January blizzard, both at night.

Tonight's journey home was one of the more pleasant. The rain had
stopped, the sky had cleared and the light on the fields had a soft lustre
that cancelled out all menace.

As I drove into Whittlesey I found myself going over very familiar
ground, for it was along this road that I was brought as a child to experience for the first time the magnetic pull of this land. Here I discovered the

world around me. It was real and unending. Pheasants, skylarks, lapwings, rabbits and hedgehogs were all part of each daily walk and it never occurred to me that life was different anywhere else. My family had worked on this land for generations and perhaps I was being shown it in preparation for the day when I too would have to start work.

Looking back at the town from which my mother and I had walked I used to feel strangely removed from all that went on there. I belonged, yet did not belong. It was like being released from the narrow street and yet still being kept on its leash. The town always looked securely packed between the tall spire of St Mary's church and the square tower of St Andrew's. It was the only town I knew. It was an island surrounded by nothing but fields and fields.

When I reached the railway crossing again (which is now controlled automatically from some remote signal-box) my thoughts went back to those days when we used to stop and talk to the old gate-keeper. If we stayed long enough the little bells in his hut would start chirping out their secret messages and he would limp outside to close the gates ready for the next train to pass through. Even before the train came into sight I could hear the sound of its wheels pre-echoing along the shining rails.

There was no magic left now. The little hut was boarded up and bind-weed had strangled the flower-bed outside the door. Driving back into the street where I was born I felt disappointed that it all looked so ordinary, so small and different. I thought of the shock I'd had a year before when I walked into it accidentally and saw a bulldozer knocking down our old house, not only our house but all the others in the row. My first reaction was one of sadness, then acceptance and finally relief. Those houses were nothing to be proud of in the twentieth century, nothing to get senti-mental about. But I knew then, as I felt now, that it was from that house that I began my first excursions into the fens and grew to love the country-side at the end of our street. I could have walked away but I was curious to see what the house would look like half knocked down, curious to see what my reactions would be looking again into those tiny rooms after thirty years. Clouds of dust blew across the road as another wall fell. For a moment I stopped, then, with a child's morbid curiosity that draws him to gloat for a moment over a dead animal, I walked closer and stood on the opposite side of the road to watch the last wall crumble, the dust settle, the men throw a door on to a heap of burning wood. Through this gap in the street I could see what used to be our garden.

Looking at that patch of ground a year later I am still surprised that so much happened there. Now the land is derelict and three broken-down cars fill up the space where four families lived. All the shops, the trades-men, the pubs and chapels that made that street so self-sufficient have gone or have been changed into different houses. But the swifts still race noisily up and down, reminding me of summer nights a long time ago when the pavements would be lined with men sitting on door-steps or wooden chairs, tired men enjoying the evening's coolness after a hot day in the brickyards.

As usual it was a mistake to look back, a mistake to expect the feelings of thirty years ago to still be there. The sensations I had as a child could only exist where they began, in the imagination. Reality and memory are frequently in conflict. I should have been satisfied with what I prefer to remember.

Night Again

For the second night I walk through the deserted streets of my home town and am surprised at the changes that are being made. Already the outskirts of town have lost their fields to new housing estates and the population has grown from 9,000 to 11,000 in the last ten years. But now the centre of the old town is changing too. Streets lose familiar landmarks. Old houses disappear.

I see tonight that they are pulling down the old Queen's Head, a public house that did not always enjoy a good reputation but had quite a history. I remember Edmund Blunden telling me that it was the inn where he stayed in the 1920s when he was working on the Clare manuscripts in Peterborough Museum. He could not get accommodation in the city because all the hotels and lodging houses were crowded for the Horse Fair, so he used to walk the seven miles at the end of each day to sleep here in this uncomfortable inn.

He wrote about his experience in an essay entitled "Wills and Testa-ments" published in his book *The Face of England* in 1932:

We were led along the flagged passage, up twisting staircases to some garrets, all beams and shadows, with the noise of starlings and sparrows bustling in the roof overhead. Two centuries behind the world.... The floor had hollows in it, the palliasses had fleas in them. Here we lived many days, and in the long living-room ... would recollect the Fens and some who had spoken of our poet. ...

It was an inn used by casual labourers and gypsies who had parked their caravans in the yard at the back. It was here where Edmund Blunden was asked to witness the last will and testament of a rat-poisoner dying of throat cancer, a man whose only possession was his horse and cart which he bequeathed to the landlord—"a man who had grown into almost the shape and colour of a pollard willow".

There are many memories and stories associated with the inn but they, like the echoes of Edmund Blunden's experiences there, will soon be lost forever under the rubble and foundations of a new building. The gypsies and their caravans have departed, the last thirsty labourers have put down their glasses and gone. The roof is already off and the windows smashed in. By the time this chapter is finished the whole building will be down. A piece more of the old town will have disappeared, and some rejoice while others regret.

I spend the rest of the evening with my parents who now live in a house converted from another pub that wasn't pulled down and still retains some memories of what its life was like. Remnants from its past often come to light when repairs are being carried out, or the garden is being dug. Dozens of old clay 'churchwarden' pipes have come to the surface in recent years, together with decorated coat-hooks, old coins and bottles.

We sit in what used to be the Smoke Room and my father starts to remember the life of the town sixty and seventy years ago. He tells me of some of the annual events that governed their lives then, such as Plough Witch Monday, when, at the beginning of the year a group of six men would pull a plough round the town threatening to pull up people's door-steps if they did not contribute a copper or two to their collecting-box. Sometimes the men would dress up in costume and always they would be pursued by a crowd of children. This was followed the next day by a ritual, almost unique to Whittlesey, known as Straw Bear Tuesday. Then a man dressed completely in straw danced through the streets with another man collecting what money they could for the farmworkers to spend on bread and beer.

I heard again about the Whittlesey Statutes Fair, when farm labourers were put up for a year's hire, and how the market square would be full of men hoping for work. The strongest men obviously went first and to the best farmers, who were usually also the most honest masters, leaving the weaker looking to be picked up by more unscrupulous men.

These Fairs had arrived in England before Christianity and became the traditional feasts on which to seek for employment or, as their origins suggest, for the landowners to hire their workers. The Statutes Fair (usually pronounced "stattus" locally) had been part of English rural life for nearly 600 years, from when a statute was passed in 1352 to provide a means of labour exchange "owing to the shortage of labourers following the Black Death".

The Fairs still come to the Market Square at the same time of year but now they are, fortunately, for amusement only, and the only creatures that appear to suffer any humiliation are the pathetic little goldfish in plastic bags containing no more than two inches of water.

Hospital Sundays and United Sunday School Anniversaries and Outings were also part of a life that satisfied itself for generations with the rough, simple pleasures of an independent community. There were always individuals who stood out, more for their nonsense or foolishness than anything else. People could laugh at a neighbour, who might be "three bricks short of a load", without any malice. My father thought of a neighbour from his childhood, a man who was the father of twins and, when they died, said in all seriousness that he could only afford to go into mourning for one. He meant it, just as much as the man who said that the first time he went up a ladder was down a well. Only the other week I heard an old man passing on a reliable home-cure remedy for a bad cough. 'Yew can take that from me,' he said after explaining what to do, 'that that's the finest cure there is for a cough, and I should know 'cus I've 'ad one for thirty-five years.'

Gypsies had shared several of their remedies with the local people years ago and one that apparently worked without harmful results was warm hedgehog oil from a hedgehog that had recently been cooked in clay over an open fire. Pig's lard was used for dandruff and dry hair. Dandelion roots were eaten to purify the blood. A roast mouse was supposed to be good for whooping-cough, or a walk round the gas-works when they were cleaning out the retorts. Senna and rhubarb were good for 'relaxing the bowels' and cayenne pepper good for heart-burn. Teething infants were given a dose of laudanum to make them sleep, and the local blacksmith was sometimes called upon to act as the dentist as well as the maker of horseshoes.

The muffled death-bell of the church announced to the town its latest loss—three strokes for a man; five strokes for a woman, followed by a toll of the bell for every year of the deceased's life. That is a custom I can still remember and it continued even after we'd lost our town-crier who used to go round calling out the name of the person for whom the bell had tolled.

A different bell was the Workmen's Bell that was rung every morning at five o'clock to rouse the men for work. The Bellman's fee was paid for each year from the rents received from the parish allotments. Now, new housing estates stand where the allotments were and only the street names are left to remind us of that old custom.

No evening goes quicker than when the old tales come out again for an airing and my mind is busy with all the memories I've heard of lamp-lighters, bloater-men and pig-killers as I walk out once more into the dark and silent night. The air is still quite warm. The smell from the honeysuckle over the door fills the darkness with unbelievable sweetness.

I cross the road and pass the ground where my grandparents' house used to stand. Immediately it comes back to me with the echoes of voices and the shadows of rooms now gone. I remember especially that day when, as a child, I stayed with my grandmother while my parents went to London.

It was an old house surrounded by a garden and trees that made me think, in those days, that my grandparents lived in a park. Their house stood caged in branches and a net of ivy, like a forsaken castle. The path to it, I thought, was as long as our street. Inside, the rooms were full of interesting objects. There was not an empty corner to be found. Glass domes of stuffed birds stood on the sideboard or in the window. Orna-ments stood on the mantelpiece beside the clock. There was grandfather's old gramophone, a stuffed animal I always think of as a fox, a case of butterflies, a box full of sepia coloured photographs, a tea-caddy full of sweet humbugs and some pictures on the wall of the First World War—everything, in fact, that a grandchild wanted. The pantry shelves had a collection of herbs, sauces and jams that fascinated me. The kitchen smelt of apples and geraniums. The dog slept under the table and chickens strutted contentedly about the yard or laid their eggs under a bush near the front door. There was coloured glass in one of the windows that made the sunlight look different. There was a swing on an apple tree that made flights into the sky possible, and there were outbuildings full of secrets. I didn't want my parents to come back from London too soon. When they did it was nearly midnight and I was fast asleep on a black leather sofa. The memory of the cold night air on my face as I was carried home comes back to me now with such vividness that I put my hand to my cheeks to feel them.

But the house and all its secrets has gone. It fell down years ago and the garden has been fenced off and built on again. All that remains is a chestnut tree planted by my eldest aunt eighty years ago when she was a child. Each year I come to watch the new leaves spring from the sticky knuckles on the bough and then wait, first for the opening hand of leaves and then for the candle blossoms to burn for their brief life. Their flames are out now and in a few months' time they will be replaced by the burning leaves of autumn that, in their turn will fall to add their dust to the roots and ruins of many years.

The town clock chimes and I count the strokes. It is again midnight.

A Few Days Later

Sauntering through any small town or village it is surprising how many remnants of other times remain, not only the obvious ones like churches, bridges, names of streets and old market squares, but less obvious ones like notices left on walls, things found in junk-yards, bits and pieces overlooked by time.

Today I keep seeing signs that I've never noticed before. The fading lettering on the gable end of an old house, letters that have been whitewashed over more than once but which still say "GOOD STABLES HERE". The high-water mark cut into a brick wall a hundred and fifty years ago when the street used to be flooded in winter. The gateway at the side of another converted inn which still has its cobbled path and boot-scraper against the front door. A disused village pump and a horse-trough planted with geraniums. Post-boxes bearing the royal initials "VR" and old gaslights bracketed on alley walls. All survivors of the many changes that have come to each community and each one like an old photograph come to life.

I am going to Impington Village College to work with a group of children who are interested in writing. It is a bright morning and I keep to the less busy roads that take me over the fens rather than use the main carriageways that would get me there quicker. I travel once again along Forty Foot Drain towards Chatteris, a town that once had more than sixty pubs for a population of 5,000. The streets are already busy with shoppers, walking quite soberly now that the town is down to about three or four modest inns.

I drive towards Mepal, to Sutton-in-the-Isle and on to Haddenham. There is a strong cross breeze, enough to bend the hedges over and sweep the white clouds quickly across the sky. A gull gets blown like a piece of paper over a beach of barley. Poppies on the roadside shake like soundless bells, their bright scarlet notes ringing among the grass. In the distance I can see Ely cathedral, but I turn off the road to Ely and take the one that is called Twentypence Road, to Cottenham.

Soon the landscape loses its flatness and there are several attractive contours in the fields that rise away from the fens. Hand-made notices appear at regular intervals along the roadside where small farmhouses try to catch what passing trade they can—BROWN EGGS; FREE RANGE EGGS; THE WORLD'S BEST EGGS; FRESH CUT BEANS; HOME-GROWN TATERS; PULL YOUR OWN. . . . Buckets of flowers stand outside some of the cottage doors. But trade won't be very brisk this morning, I am the only traveller on the road at the moment, and I pass by.

When I cross the river at the Twenty Pence Inn I stop the car and get out to enjoy a few moments of the fresh air, the free-range air that doesn't need pulling, the fresh air that is home-grown and the best this side of north Norfolk, if not in the world.

There is a man working at the far end of the field against which I have parked. He was there the last time I came this way and that was in beet-hoeing time. Is he always there? Does he never go home?

There is something about a beet-hoer that reminds one of the timelessness of work on the land, even though the sugar-beet is a relative newcomer to English fields. It is the solitariness of the job, the steady, patient hoeing up and down the long rows, working earth's largest tapestry. The machine has not yet killed off the beet-hoer. He was there last spring and he will return. A suitable occupation for a monk, I would have thought, or a transcendentalist, but not a 'fen-tiger'.

Five minutes later I leave him to his labour as I think about my work at Impington.

There is a strange story about a woman of Impington. Her name was Elizabeth Woodcock and she was born in 1756. She was married and had eleven children. One Saturday, 2 February 1799, she rode on horseback into Cambridge to do her shopping. It was a cold day and threatened snow; by the time she had collected all her provisions it was getting towards evening and the first flakes of snow were beginning to fall. Before leaving the city she decided to call in at "The Three Tuns" for a glass or two of gin to help keep out the cold, but by the time she went to continue her journey the wind was blowing the snow into a blizzard and she was frightened. About half a mile from home she decided to take a short cut along a bridle path: at that moment the horse she was riding was startled by something and threw Elizabeth to the ground. Before she could regain her senses the horse had run off leaving her, slightly muzzy and with a load of groceries she could not carry, stranded in the snow. To collect her wits and her breath she sat under a hedge where she became heedless of the drifting snow piling up all round her. It fell so thickly that soon she was imprisoned in a cave as cold and secure as any prison. When it stopped snowing the stars came out and the snow was frozen. She was trapped for eight days before the red handkerchief that she had managed to push through a hole in the snow wall was spotted by one of the searchers. It was Sunday, 10 February, and soon a party of men were digging at the frozen drift to get her weak and frost-bitten body out. She was taken home and put to bed, but slowly her fingers and toes began to waste away, she survived another five months then, on 11 July 1799, she died at the age of forty-three. Under the official story entered in the parish register an anonymous hand wrote: "She was in a state of intoxication when she was lost. . . . Her death was accelerated (to say the least) by spiritous liquors afterwards taken, procured by the donations of numerous visitors."

So, whether Mrs Woodcock was finally killed by kindness or from the wounds of her ordeal we shall never know. She was buried in the village churchyard without a stone to mark her grave and her husband and the children left the district. Someone was telling me the other day that there is a stone marking the place where she sheltered but I have not found it yet. Perhaps I might today, or some other day, when I have time to spare.

The Impington of today is quite a different village—I mean in size and character—and has one of the most excellent Village Colleges in the country. So far I have not had to face a blizzard to get there and I can think of one or two places where I'd rather shelter if, next winter, I'm tempted to take something to keep out the cold.

The morning goes well. I am no longer surprised by the high quality of work the children produce each week. We spend more than two hours together and their writing, like their conversation, is again lively, original and stimulating. Some of their lines have an exciting freshness about them. I think of Helen's verse about fear:

> Fear is a slide before we are sliding.
> Fear is a tree we have climbed too high.
> Fear is the highest board at the swimming-pool.
> Fear is the terrible thing in the mind.

or the quiet description of clouds by Frances:

> Grey, still and tranquil,
> They cage us,
> Keep us,
> And look over us . . .

or Eric's description of a desert:

> The dry, harsh wind picks up the gritty grains of sand
> and hurls them upwards . . .
> The still water of the oasis jumps under the impact
> of the rain of sand.

We have been working hard this morning in preparation for a "Writers' Workshop" we are going to record next week at the BBC as part of a Schools Broadcast programme. The youngsters are excited and confident. What it is to be thirteen or fourteen and to be fearless of microphones.

Time goes so quickly I can't believe that it is half-past twelve when Mrs Williams comes into the room to end our 'workshop' for another week. We have forgotten how bright the day is outside, how lucky we are to be working in a comfortable room with armchairs and tables, and a window that looks out on to grass and trees. We collect our books and manuscripts and I leave, elated and exhausted, their new poems still ringing in my ears, their eagerness still filling me with joy and gratitude.

Too happy to go straight home and back to my own words I park the car in a farm gateway and sit on the grass at the edge of a wheatfield. The sun is high above me. Only a few clouds occasionally shade its power. The earth smells good. Butterflies flap from one wildflower to another and the rustle of corn sways backwards and forwards with the rhythm of water lapping on a shore. I stretch out full-length on the grass and, feeling very contented, close my eyes to sleep. . . .

. . . Twenty minutes later I was woken by a crashing wave of wind through the corn. The lazy sound that had lulled me to sleep suddenly had a much more threatening quality. I jumped up, believing for a moment that I had been caught by the in-coming tide. I looked over the field. The heavy ears of wheat were being bent over by the wind and were then springing back again only to be brushed down once more by a wind that was now stirring little clouds of dust from the cart-tracks. It was cooler too and my skin, burning from the earlier sun, suddenly shivered.

I drove back to the main road and called at a pub in Cottenham just in time to get a bar lunch. Behind, or beneath, the noisy talk a vulgarized version of Beethoven's Ninth Symphony was being played on those sentimental violins usually reserved for Palm Court Orchestras or romantic movies. The tempo had been changed and there were alien sounds coming from the percussion section. One of the customers saw me staring in amazement at the speaker above my head. 'Do you like classical music?' he asked. I felt I wasn't telling a lie when I said 'yes', and I suppose the choice could have been worse. In any case I'd not gone there for a symphony concert but for food and drink, both of which I thoroughly enjoyed.

The Gatherings

By the end of July the first fields of harvest are being gathered in, not in sheaves and wagon-loads but by the huge combines that reduce a half-year's growth to stubble and send off the grain to be dried and stored, all in a day or two, depending on the size of the field. Two or three weeks is usually enough to see all the harvests in and the fields being prepared for next year.

By the beginning of August harvesting is an activity that can be seen in most parts of the fen country, even though this land is more famous for its root crops of potatoes, sugar-beet and carrots. A summer harvest scene is still one of the best sights in the country. It brings with it a sense of fulfilment and reward for all the waiting as well as the work; it is a farming-scene most easily shared by people who have no other interest in the land. Often the waiting can be the most frustrating and destroying aspect of all. Deciding when to cut, how soon or how late, can make all the difference to a man's feelings about harvest. A day too late, and the August weather can break bringing thunder-storms and flattened crops. A day or two too soon, and you can miss another twenty hours of hot sunshine. It's a dangerous game playing with the fickle English weather.

The weather has been like that today, first one thing, then another. The morning was warm and bright but by mid-day there were signs that a change was on the way. An hour before the thunder came the clouds grew dark and the light on the fields became brilliant, as if lit from beneath. I stood and watched the sky lower into a heavy blue-purple and the ripe wheatfields shone, not so much with gold but with a rich auburn sheen, like beaten copper. Then suddenly the sky was split open by lightning and was followed by the first rockfall of thunder. The explosion shattered the clouds and rain fell like splintered glass. It crashed down with a fierceness that was frightening.

I hurried back to the car and sat there wondering whether I would ever get out again. The metal roof gave me protection from the rain and I just hoped that the four rubber tyres would be some safeguard against the lightning. All I could do was to sit and watch.

Each drop of rain that hit the road bounced back again in a shower of smaller drops. For split seconds they created wings, or sails. They became an armada of small ships sailing through the cliffs of cornfields. Helen, Frances or Eric would have come up with a good phrase to describe a storm like this, I thought.

I looked at the corn, expecting to see it slowly being beaten flat, the months of waiting, hoping, expectation, all destroyed in half an hour. But the stalks stood stiff and firm. The rain streamed down, straight as steel-rods. There was no wind to slant it one way or the other. This, so a farmer told me later, was what saved the crops from being flattened. The rain was vertical and even the fields of barley withstood its pounding. The thunder followed closer on the heels of each lightning flash and when the storm raged overhead the sky was so dark that visibility was reduced by half. A car came towards me, its headlights on, its wheels making enough spray for it to look more like a hovercraft.

Nowhere could have been more terrifying this side of an awful disaster. If the world is ever going to end then it will not produce a more awesome prelude. Indeed, perhaps this is it, I thought, coming in all its fury and ferocity. I waited for twenty minutes as the storm continued and it felt a long time to wait for the day of wrath, for the earth to finally burst into a million fragments and fall into space. When the rain suddenly eased and the sky brightened it was almost an anti-climax.

As the days pass you can see just how much luck there is in farming. That angry thunderstorm has unsettled the weather and each day knows some rain. Sometimes it is only a half-hearted drizzle, sometimes it's a sequence of short showers and today it is a continual downpour again. Not only is it raining but there is a strong wind blowing now and those crops that were standing firm a few days ago are this time being beaten down. Those farmers who have been able to make an early start to their harvesting must be sighing with relief and gratitude to know that some of their corn is in. Those who haven't been able to make a start, or who hesitated, must be cursing the weather for breaking so soon.

It's a great disappointment, even to an observer, when the final act is reduced like this to a damp squib. When you've watched a field being ploughed, sown, then grow and ripen to fullness, there is a strong wish to share in the excitement of the day when the combine-harvesters roll in to begin cutting. I hate being away from this landscape in August, for to miss the harvest, to come home and find the fields empty, is like walking out of a theatre before the play is over.

But it is too soon to be talking about this year's harvest being a damp squib. There are several weeks to go before the scene changes so completely and a few days of August heat will make all the difference. These fens will be active with harvest now for at least the next fortnight as the huge fields are cut one after another. It's a sight we take very much for granted and we cannot always appreciate the amazement of visitors who are used to farming in hill-country or, worse still, are not used to seeing any farming scenes at all. This is land which, in a good year, can yield 3 tons of wheat to the acre and 14 tons of potatoes. It's a land worth seeing and being grateful for, as we try to meet the growing demands of a population that needs more and more food.

Travelling by road or rail in the fens you soon realize that you are mostly well above the level of the fields. It is one of the features of our countryside, like the complex of waterways. A journey over the fens, especially by train, offers almost an aerial view as you look over the fields for as many miles as the eye can see. Fifty years ago the activity would have looked frenzied by today's standards for the harvest-time then was something in which most country people had a part to play. Even the trades people were glad when harvest-time came because it meant that families who had lived 'on the slate' all through winter and spring could pay off some of their debts.

I was looking at some old sepia photographs the other evening and the fields seemed to have as many land-workers on them as sheaves of wheat. The most modern piece of equipment was the binder and in several of the pictures there were teams of horses used for carting the corn to the yards for threshing. These horses were turned out as proudly as if they were being entered in an agricultural show, their manes braided, their brasses shining.

A lot of the old farmers still miss having their horses on the land. One said to me not so long ago, 'You can't talk to tractors,' and this was also a feeling expressed by another farmer writing to me from New Zealand, he too spoke of the lack of company and communication that he felt when the tractors took over the ploughing in New Zealand. Every page of his long letter was interesting, especially as he can clearly remember his childhood and early years on the land when his country was still emerging from its pioneering era:

'I have been in New Zealand 72 years and all that time has been spent on the land, first on sheep and cattle stations and, for the last 40 years fruit-growing. My memory goes back to the days when New Zealand was really in the pioneering stages in the back-blocks; no roads, no phones, no railways, but just bullock waggons, stage-coaches and pack-horses. The mail came once a week, the doctors and parsons visited on horseback; we had bush-fires, floods and droughts. It was all hard work. Yet we were happy, we knew no better. . . .

'Part of my job on the sheep and cattle stations was as a plowman and waggoner. They were joyful years, all alone with my six horses, to whom I sang and recited. I was even vain enough to think that they enjoyed it. Cattle do like music and song, it seems to give them a sense of security. When the tractors came in, about 1925, song was not quite the same. They had no ear for my song, but the purring of the engine did at least drown my many false notes. Oh I enjoyed those days of grooming and caring for my horses. . . .'

I have heard several men say that horses like a good song and I also know a man near Chatteris who works on the land and can remember when he used to sing ballads to his cattle or make up rhymes to amuse himself as he worked alone all day. He still does, I suppose, and when he talks of an evening's poaching or wildfowling he talks "poetry". But he will never read it. "I've ed no education for books," he'll say, "and as for poetry, good lork-a-day, boy, that's something I'll never understand."

My grandfather, who could not read or write, had a great wealth of folklore and a natural ear for melody. He started work at the age of seven tending sheep for fourpence a day, but he could tell you all about the seasons of the year, the phases of the moon, the times of high-tide, the haunts of wild animals, which herbs to use for cures and where to find mushrooms. What more do you need to know?

But I was going to say, before I got on to horses and other diversions, that it is too soon to be talking about the end of this year's harvest. For the next few days, in any direction, you will see half a dozen combines suddenly appearing like creatures from outer-space to gnaw their way through acres of ripe corn. And once again the fields will be full of activity as these machines move slowly, for there is still a feeling of celebration even in a modern harvest field. Harvest will always be harvest and there is no greater pleasure than watching the gathering, no greater satisfaction than seeing the fields cut, the grain threshed and transferred from the combine into the waiting trailers—a waterfall of brown wheat that smells of all the summers the earth has ever known. At the end of the day the baled straw is collected and stacked, and the corn-stubble is left for burning.

Until recently the burning of stubble could be one of the most dramatic sights in the fens, particularly at nights when the flames roared slowly across the dark fields and could be seen from miles away. But now it is against regulations to burn at night because tighter restrictions are being imposed to reduce the risk of unattended fires spreading and getting out of hand.

There are always arguments about whether it's good farming or not to set fire to a field at the end of harvest. I used to feel it was a suitably ritualistic ceremony to complete the season by turning the stubble into camp-fires and torches, but I'm not so sure now. One responds less and less to the extrovert acts of man in nature and I shall be satisfied to see the fields empty, the gates closed, the plans for another year not revealed for a while. The land needs frost as well as fire and winter can do the land as much good in some ways. The burning of the stubble is not only seen as dangerous now but also as wasteful. Recent experiments have shown that the straw can now be turned into valuable animal food. A report that has just been published estimates that by burning off four million tons of straw each harvest British farmers are destroying in a few weeks material which contains as much energy as the one-and-three-quarter million tons of oil they use directly in accomplishing the rest of their farming operations. At Nottingham University experiments have been carried out which show that as much as 20 per cent of the cereal grains that are used in feeding beef cattle and dairy cows could be replaced by the barley straw that is mostly burnt on the fields. Although cattle is not a prime consideration in fen-farming the rapidly increasing costs of keeping cattle make all farmers very conscious of saving and utilizing what they can to help keep prices down. Stubble-fires may soon be a harvest scene as dated as the hand-gathered sheaves.

Another Time

A picture appeared in our local newspaper this week of a skeleton that had just been discovered on the outskirts of the town. It was of a teenage girl, complete even to the thirty-two teeth still in the skull. Foul-play could not be ruled out, but as the girl died 3,000 years ago it may be difficult to provide the necessary evidence.

The story reminded me again of how casually we pass over history. I pass the field where this Bronze Age girl was found as many as three hundred times a year. It's on one of the roads that lead to the North Bank of the Nene, where the farming land takes over from the factories, or I should say where the factories are beginning to take over the fields.

It is not the first archaeological find of such interest in the area and I knew that excavation work had been carried out before on the edge of Flag Fen. The site has produced remains of settlements from as far back as the Neolithic age. But the skeleton of that girl really caught my imagination. She had only been lying six feet under the soil where I had picked wild flowers and stood many times listening to skylarks. Surely I ought to have heard whispers, or seen a ghost or two at nights? Surely I ought to have known there was someone about? On her right hand she wore a double-stranded bronze ring. Was she married, or engaged? If so, to whom?

The dig was being carried out by a team of archaeologists from America, Canada and England. They have many more acres to cover before the site becomes drowned under a new flood of industrial development, before we bury part of our own history. The girl's skeleton, though more romantic, reminded me of the bog-oaks I had seen and written about a year before:

> Had you been carved into the image of a king
> or sacred animal from some lost dynasty,
> thousands would come to stare through glass
> at your antiquity. But black and rotting
> by this fenland dyke you stay ignored—
> the trunks of trees ploughed up from this dark soil
> that kept your secret for six thousands years
> while our brief histories were shed like leaves
> upon your long-forgotten, unmarked graves.
>
> We call you 'bog-oaks', though you were seldom such;
> your bark fine-grained, your inner wood, when cut,
> as raw as meat. What world was yours, we ask,
> before catastrophes of ice, wind, storm and flood
> brought you so low to lie beneath this mud?
> What lord or tribe once strolled beneath your leaves
> before the pyramids took shape or emperors ruled?
> Did you know lovers once as well as huntsmen
> and conspirators? Perhaps. Some pride seems left.

But think how hard it is for us to comprehend
that you once lived before the age of Pharaohs
and of Christ, or that your leaves once danced
before Salome, or the fall of Greece.
So much has gone since your boughs blossomed then
that, seeing you dumped upon this muddy bank,
we hurry past with no thought of your times,
no knowledge of your glories, rituals, fears,
no reverence for your fallen gods or kings.

I go out in the early evening to see if I can find and feel again this spirit
of antiquity, the spirits of tribal lords and a people who were here long
before us and left this land for someone else's history. But nothing happens. There is no tense atmosphere or magic tonight. A few cows graze in
one field, beyond them the brickyard chimneys lean like old men puffing
smoke into the sultry air. Perhaps I am trying too hard. I am trying to
create the spirit I want rather than wait patiently for the land itself to
speak.

I go back into Peterborough and walk the streets for an hour with no
real purpose in mind, trying to get used to the noise of traffic again, trying
to fit myself into my own times. Familiar landmarks look strange and
different. New landmarks no longer jar but melt into the uninspiring
backcloth of the shopping centre. After thinking about the Bronze Age
girl and the Neolithic times before her, our 'old' and 'new' become
one.

I walk into the cathedral precincts. The evening sunlight warms that
glorious West Front so that even those stones look new. Two thousand
years were to pass between that girl dying and those stones being erected.
I walk round the outside of the great building and can see beyond the trees
a new block of flats rising to a similar height. There was some trouble in
the beginning about that monument to the Seventies going up. I remember
a conversation I had one wet Sunday morning with an American archaeologist who was working on the site. What did he think about the changes
we were making?

'But things are always changing, aren't they?' he said. 'People are
always having to make way for someone. Did you know for instance that
this site was once a Deer Park for the Abbot of Medeshamstede?'

I knew that the city had once had that name and that earlier monastic buildings had stood where the cathedral now stands, but I'd not given much thought to whether the abbot had a Deer Park or not.

'Well,' continued the man from Illinois, 'he had to destroy a village to make room for his deer, 'and where did the people go? Don't ask me. You could ask, where did the deer go, or the abbot for that matter? All I know is I have about eight hours left to work on this site. Tomorrow the concrete arrives and then, brother, we shan't know a thing about any of it. It's how quickly some things go that worries me . . . twelve hundred years are nothing, but you come here in a week's time and tell me where they've gone.'

I remember looking at the muddy ground beneath my feet. Those little squares of charcoal in the wet, sandy trenches, had they really been fires on someone's hearth?

The American had worked on sites in Tunbridge Wells and Winchester and was going on to Grantham in the morning. History for him was a series of small wastelands where soon the concrete would arrive and new buildings would bury his patient work.

Our conversation ended and he bent down again to scrape away at the soil. I remember looking over to the grey cathedral that morning and realizing for the first time that there was a time when it hadn't stood there, it made the funeral of Katharine of Aragon seem like only yesterday. Those weather-beaten figures on the eastern building could have been damaged and deformed by vandals in an hour, rather than by the weather of centuries.

But now my concept of Time becomes blurred again. This ancient church has the power to stretch the years, to offer some degree of permanence. The vision and craftsmanship of those workmen who built and fashioned these stones into something so lasting may have the laugh on us yet.

In a landscape where there are no hills you need something like Peterborough cathedral, or Ely cathedral, or even Crowland abbey, to defy Time.

The Warm Days

Summer has reached its peak and the last days of August have brought the weather we always believe we had in the summers of our childhood. We can forget the storms and relax again in the hot lazy air of an afternoon that dismisses winter and the threat of Judgement Day from our minds.

Tall hollyhocks and gladioli now brighten the gardens. A sultry stillness comes to the village streets and the fens have the limp quietness of the sea when the tide is out.

Although these warm days lull us into lethargy there are subtle signs that autumn is not far away. I sit writing in the garden soon after breakfast and notice that the grass is glistening with dew and is covered with small squares of grey cobwebs. When I rub my hand over the grass my fingers become as wet as if I had dipped them into a pool.

A Red Admiral butterfly almost settles on my writing-pad and then goes off towards a foam of pink phlox. The garden is very still. I look up into the sky. It is pale blue and cloudless, very high and empty. The emptiness makes me realize that the swifts have already left us and their swirling flight-patterns are absent from the air above me.

When did they go? Surely they were there yesterday? Is it their sudden absence that gives the morning its unexpected stillness? Why did they leave just when we look like having a heat-wave? Do they know better? Have they measured their journey and know it would be unwise to stay for our bonus summer?

Soon the house-martins and the swallows will follow the cuckoo and the swifts and we shall begin to look for the in-coming birds presaging a different season. Soon the blue-tits and the wren will be back in the garden looking for their usual supply of food.

I noticed yesterday when I was out that the chestnut trees are already looking quite yellow and tattered, their leaves half-rusted away before the boys have even picked up the first conkers or pitched their sticks up into the branches to encourage their fall.

There is a wood-pigeon close by, his soft, throaty cooing adding drowsiness to the warm air. I look up again at the empty sky and at the same moment a heron flies over. He looks out of place up there, flapping slowly under the hot sun and so far from the water. After the speed of the swifts his flight is lumbering and unnatural. He looks so slow and alone he could be a solitary camel crossing that desert of cloudless sky. Which oasis is he looking for I wonder? He must change direction if he's looking for the River Nene otherwise he will fly over what for him will be a wasteland, the sprawling city and its suburbs—unless of course he knows one or two well-equipped gardens where there is a good supply of gold-fish. But he flaps on until he becomes a speck in the far distance and the ornamental ponds on the edge of town are safe this morning.

It's no good, there are too many distractions outside for me to get any work done. I must go indoors and face the typewriter again. It's not a pleasant thought, but the day will have little to show for itself in a month's time if I don't.

The day ended with a remarkable sunset, even by fen-country standards. The clouds grew like a coral reef on the edge of the world. Particles, sections, layers and shelves of brilliant colours turned the sky into a great wonder. There was no modesty about today's sunset. It was an ostentatious display of theatrical splendour. It heralded a tournament between the day and night. Bright flags of many royal shades were draped across the fields. The clouds shone so much you could *hear* their colours and lesser clouds on the edge of the crowd echoed their fanfares. The space beyond the gaudy array of orange, red, purple and green was a rich bright blue. The sun itself could not be seen but hid, like some great but temperamental actor, in the wings, waiting to make a big entrance or, in this production, a grand exit. People not used to taking much notice of sunsets came out into their gardens or stood at their doors to see the sky burning, to gasp in awe that such things still happened in the world of nature. Colour television could not compete. We stood in our gardens or at bedroom windows watching the oldest show on earth.

For my money I would have liked to have been on the North Bank or Deeping High Bank to witness such a leave-taking. From either vantage point you have an enormous expanse of low land and vast skies. There would have been nothing to restrict the impact of seeing acres of space put on such a stunning act. We were lucky that the elements had bred such a cast of clouds during the afternoon for this evening's performance.

For a sunset to happen the clouds and the sun have to be in the right place at the right time of day. It would be no use the sun hanging about on the horizon without the sky's mirrors to reflect its late burning. Nor will it work if the clouds are so dark the light cannot pierce through each waiting spectrum. One breath of wind can spoil the whole evening. Conditions have to be right, even for miracles.

A Different Silence

I like entering churches when I know they are empty, or perhaps I should say when I'm alone and there's no service in progress. The walk up to the church door, the moment of anticipation wondering whether the door will be locked, the turn of the handle, the click of the latch, the echoing sound from inside and the smell of the church as the door opens; then the first few steps and the inevitable glance round, looking for the unexpected, for something different.

Some churches surprise, many disappoint. Some have a quality of calm and age that you can feel immediately you enter, others give the impression that they are there only to perform the rituals of the parish—the weddings, christenings, funerals, and occasional service for the few who wish to attend.

Some churches accept and encompass, closing a warm, safe silence around you so that the body's tensions drain away and your whole being becomes relaxed. It is a joy to sit there in the stillness—whatever one's belief—to absorb the power of stone and prayer, to let the years speak and the captured light heal. Others fail to meet any need at all and send one hurriedly away from their cold atmosphere in search of something else.

What is it that gives some buildings this degree of power, or influence, this "spirit of place"? Why are some able to draw us in and offer safe harbour whilst others look down upon us as unwelcome intruders?

There are churches of both kinds in the fens. Some I pass by knowing that I shall not enjoy stopping there. Others I can visit again and again, knowing that at any time of the day or year I shall be able to sit there for a while and come away lighter in soul and body.

It does not have to be an impressive building with unique features— though St Wendreda's at March with its famous Hammerbeam Angel roof, or St Kyneburga's with one of the finest Norman towers in the country, or those churches at Holbeach, Helpringham, Boston and Bourne all justly claim such praise and cannot be passed by; no, even the most modest village church can offer something that others cannot, a feeling of continuity and importance in the lives of people who have lived there generation after generation.

I have my favourites throughout the fens of Lincolnshire and Cambridgeshire, in Marshland and Norfolk. I think immediately of South Creake, Walpole St Peter, Northborough, Werrington and Crowland.

The abbey at Crowland especially always gives me something, whether in the church itself or among the beautiful ruins surrounding the church saved from those ruins. I've never been to a service there but I have been many times when I've felt the need of a different silence and I have always left with a sense of gratitude and serenity.

It's more than somewhere to sit and get problems into perspective; it's

more than somewhere to leave the exaggerated fears and worries of Now.
It is somewhere where you can "suddenly sail into slack water" and feel
some of life's longings answered.

> I enter again
> the stones' cool silence,
> not to affirm some whisper
> of a frail belief
> but to be still, to feel
> pale sunlight cross the floor
> or see again the dusty smell
> of waiting in the air.
>
> I want no other music
> than my loud heart's metronome,
> I have no other prayer
> unless kind peace creeps in
> behind closed eyes
> or through involuntary hands.
>
> I want no gift,
> unless that old release comes down,
> leaving within these walls
> those griefs I'd rather leave without.
> I want no more
> than what I always find
> and never can repay.

I can enter and leave this place because of a young soldier who, tired
of the vain glories of war, retired from the world of politics and fighting
to pursue a humble life of devotion here on a very lonely island.

That was in AD 699 when most of the fen country was under water and
where, apart from those scattered settlements on islands such as Ramsey,
Whittlesey, Thorney, Ely, Manea, Sutton and Croyland (or "Crulande"
as it was known), life was extremely primitive.

The young man and ex-soldier who had decided to "drop out" of court
life and senseless battles was named Guthlac. He was the son of a Mercian
nobleman by the name of Penwald, a family of wealth and status.

Guthlac had tried other abbeys before choosing to find his own plot of
land in a more challenging and inhospitable part of the country. At the

age of twenty-four he had gone to the abbey of Repton to become a monk. But the demands upon him were not enough; he believed that he had to find his own destiny, that because of what he was, more was expected of him. Two years later he came to East Anglia, to the island of Croyland, where he built his first hermit's cell and began his life of prayer and good works.

He arrived on St Bartholomew's Day in 699 and survived his first years of nightmares, ague, weather, suspicion and hostility from the natives until he became respected and sought-after by men wanting his blessing and advice.

One of these men was Prince Ethelbald, of whom Guthlac prophesied a succession to the throne of Mercia. On hearing this the Prince vowed that if the monk's words came true then he would build a great monastery on Guthlac's ground as an act of gratitude.

On 11 April 714 Guthlac died at the age of forty, but his prophecy came true and Ethelwald kept his promise. On St Bartholomew's day in 716 the king laid the foundations of the first abbey, a thanksgiving to God for the life of a wise and good man who declined the power and material wealth of this life to satisfy a far more difficult desire.

The abbey was destroyed and rebuilt, destroyed and built again, and now it stands once more in ruins—apart from the north aisle which is today's parish church. Between the eighth century and the twentieth century it has known many invaders, some in Viking long-boats, some on Cromwellian horses, sometimes by fire, sometimes by flood. There are many life-stories hidden in its shadows apart from St Guthlac's. What of Abbot Theodore, slain at the altar while praying for the souls of the marauding Danes? What of young Turgar, a thirteen-year-old boy who fled with a brother monk as the remains of the abbey fell in flames around him? What of so many people who, for a thousand years, have added their spirit to this silent place?

A few names are known, a few memories left, but the abbey's famous library of seven hundred manuscripts was destroyed in the fire of 1091. The history lost then can only now be imagined.

Not all of this history could have been so over-burdened with tragedy and disaster. Guthlac had established a 'spirit of place' that could not be destroyed and there were years of peace and achievement as well as war and destruction.

St Guthlac himself could even be called the St Francis of Croyland, for an early life of the saint written by Felix, a monk at the abbey some seventy years later, tells how he tamed birds and fishes to eat from his

D

hand. Swallows flew in through his open window to settle on his shoulders or perch on his arms. They returned to him each year and would not begin to build their nest until Guthlac had shown them the place where they might build and put there a handful of dry grass.

Pageantry must have come into the life of the abbey too, as its wealth and fame grew. In 1113 Joffrid of Orleans gave a banquet there at which five thousand people were entertained and such a gathering may not have been seen in Croyland since.

Kings came to pay their homage to the saint's island and the church that had been rebuilt and enlarged on three occasions. In 1460 Henry VI stayed for three days and nights and eight years later there was a visit from Edward IV. It was the first abbey in the country to have a tower for pealing bells and its lands were distributed throughout six counties and fifty parishes. In more recent times its bells were among the first to be broadcast in this country and its visitors now include many from overseas, from America, New Zealand, Brazil and Japan.

But although history has made Croyland what it is nothing can mar its romantic and humble beginning, or spoil the atmosphere that survives because of one unselfish man. It is his spirit that pervades and heals, his wisdom and humility that call you back.

There is a lot more to the story of Croyland (or Crowland, as it is known now) and I have told it more fully elsewhere. I mention it again because it is a very essential part of this solitary landscape and a very important part of my environment. I go many times to be there alone. I go often to take friends and visitors to get their reactions. I'm never sure how much they get from it and I have to remember that my own feelings are the accumulation of several years.

Beyond the famous Norman arch, beyond the space, beyond the graves and the boundary walls, beyond the history of twelve hundred years, the fens draw back under so many ghosts. They brood, dark and furtive, as if they still know secrets we have not heard. And they must know more for they are always there, hour after hour, year after year, always watching, seeing, listening, absorbing. We only visit.

Towards Destinations

The swallows and the martins are getting ready to leave. For the past two or three days I have noticed them congregating on the telegraph-wires, taking-off, returning, re-gathering, and then scattering again in a series of practice leave-takings.

I stop again this morning on the North Bank, near the Dog-in-a-Doublet to watch them. There are several overhead wires there that still link the farms by phone and the birds are clustered on them like notes of music, a stave of semi-quavers from a heavily-scored piano sonata.

I try counting the birds but when I get to seventy they all spring from their resting place and scatter about the sky for a few moments before returning again to the same wire. I try at least half a dozen times and, as if they're teasing me, they wait until my count is nearly finished and then flurry once more into a scribble of flight that cancels all my calculations.

I know by their numbers and their excitement that they will soon be gone, that they are preparing for a sudden departure towards destinations that make me feel very earthbound. A day or two longer perhaps, a few more trial runs and then from some signal, or instinct, they will head south and not return again until next spring. The wires will be empty, no longer the staves of a musical score but the strings of an untuned cello on which the wind will play its long winter notes.

In some ways the thought of winter excites me for I usually find myself writing well in the winter. Poems that have haunted me all summer start to take shape, ideas that have been backwards and forwards like birds begin to settle. The months of gestation are nearly over and by the time the fields are also empty and this landscape is bare I shall be writing with greater intensity than I have felt all year. It's probably only guilt for all those wasted weeks of summer but it always happens. The best writing periods always come in late October and November, the beginning of winter, and then in late February and March, the beginning of spring.

Someone said to me earlier this year, 'Why do you stay in the fens? After all, what is there in that dreary landscape to write about? You ought to break out and try Scotland for a change, or Cornwall, or even the Cotswolds!'

I took the hint, but turned my back on the setting sun and looked out over these low-lit lands for the millionth time and suddenly wondered why they looked new and undiscovered.

At Whatever Moment This Is

Looking over the fields into the distance, looking into that space between the earth and sky, feeling the infinity beyond the horizon and the clouds, I know that today is one of those days that will not fit into our pattern of Time. There is no yesterday, no tomorrow; it is not this year, or last; not BC or AD. Just—NOW.

Such feelings have come before, usually in moments of complete happiness when the mind, heart, head, in fact the entire body is content with what it has. It is a day for going deeply into one's self to have complete affinity with all that is outside. I don't know whether I'm a cloud, or a clod of earth, a bird or a wildflower; and it doesn't matter. I'm here for a moment as part of this planet and feel the rhythm of its life so perfectly harmonized with my own that there are no fears or frictions, no greeds or ambitions.

Only when this rhythm of the earth takes over are we able to feel so completely free. Only when our own individual rhythm is synchronized with that of the land and the sky, the water and the clouds, with the slow movement of the Universe, do we become whole. Only then can we strip ourselves of the material things that keep us "out of step" and prevent us from enjoying our real existence.

Rhythm enters into us through the eyes as well as the ears. We inhale it with our breath, it seeps in through our skin. Why do we respond in the way that we do to the sea, or the flow of a river, or to the wind through the grass? For ourselves to be still we perhaps need to feel the movement of the earth, the slow journey of day into night. To be static is not to be still. To sleep is not always to rest. Being totally absorbed by the conditions of a special day is to know some kind of rebirth, something approaching completeness and joy. And this is not to be selfish. After such a day our relationship with others can only be better.

And today is a special day. To a stranger, perhaps even to a friend, I might be considered selfish and lazy. Just sitting here could be thought a complete waste of time. But I know the value of what I am doing. I can feel the extreme tensions and doubts running off me again like dirt being washed away under a shower. This seems even better than being in church. At this moment I neither know the time of the day nor the day of the month. Who needs a date on such a day? The fields have been there longer than dates. The sky has no calendar. The clouds form and move

slowly away. Light will eventually give way to dark. But now, at whatever moment this is, I am happy and completely absorbed by the warmth
and the silence, by the earth and the air. I could call it "nature" but somehow that word has been devalued and is no longer strong enough to
express this real and profound relationship between a human being and his
landscape.

Again I make a rash claim: that this landscape stretches the individual's
response more than any other. No hills or mountains provide acceptable
boundaries, to put the farthest aspect within touching distance. No contours lure the eyes into one sheltered valley or leafy corner. It demands
everything. Alone on 100,000 acres of land you are no more than a seed
of grass. But the seed is also everything. What has gone before and what
may still be to come are of little importance. This Timelessness excuses,
forgives, and reconciles all.

Close the eyes, and nothing changes. Stretch out on the grass, still with
the eyes closed, and feel the slow turn of the earth. Open the eyes and the
first thing you see is the sky above you and around you. You are weight-
less, floating, turning with the world. Put out your hand and feel the
ground. It is like touching soil for the first time. It is like waking from a
dream. You float down until you feel the earth's roundabout also slowing
down. You sit up, open your eyes, and appreciate the day's light again and
the distance. You know you have never been more alive than at this
moment. Creation must have been like this, a slow turning, a slow awakening and an awareness of light, the surprise of breathing, of feeling, of
becoming part of reality.

But because we have to step back into *our* illusion of Time these
moments of reality appear unreal and the experience, or the dream, has to
be seen as part of a particular day and season. We have to return to our
calendars and the responsibilities of our civilizations. We have to compromise. We have to get up and go home, return to work and the daily
timetables, to the stacks of forms that have to be filled in for one Government department or another. We can only hope that the "moment of
unreality" will have enriched our lives sufficiently to help us withstand the
pressures that occasionally disturb the rhythm of our true personalities,
that alienate us from the perpetual creation.

Looking over the fields and into the distance, I think to myself—one
day we shall invent music and language and colours so that we shall be
able to record and preserve such moments. Sitting alone for hours and
looking into that space between the earth and sky, it is easy to forget that
Man has been dreaming of this for over 10,000 years.

Mozart, Purcell, Debussy, Messiaen; Titian, Leonardo da Vinci and Van Gogh; Sophocles, Shakespeare, Goethe and Hermann Hesse; these are the identities given by our history to the "dreaming man". They are one spirit, outside yesterday and tomorrow. One spirit, looking at this moment through a million pairs of eyes, listening with a million pairs of ears and responding with a million heart-beats.

'Now get up and go home,' I tell myself.

And it hurts to separate my hands from the grass. It hurts to tear myself away from the earth.

PART TWO

TOWARDS LEAF-FALL

―――――――――

"Methinks the reflections are never purer
and more distinct than now at the season
of the fall of the leaf ... when the evenings
grow cool and lengthen, and our winter
evenings with their bright fires may be
said to begin."

Thoreau: Oct 17th 1858

Marshlands

IF I HAD to choose I suppose I would say that the ultimate solitariness in this solitary landscape is to be found in the Marshlands of Lincolnshire and parts of north Norfolk; that apron of low land reclaimed from the sea that spreads in from the Wash. There you can feel alone without that awful feeling of loneliness. There you can be one with the earth, air and water without losing your identity.

It's a haunting place, as all marshlands are. I have been there in different seasons and have always come back with a wonderful sense of renewal and freshness. Wildness tames us.

In springtime the salty smell and light of the marshes add a new dimension to the year's beginning. In summer they are warm and languid with heat-haze and the smell of dried mud. In winter they can be Siberian with their freezing fogs or icy winds. But in autumn they are calm and rich in texture with golden colours and clear skies, with an atmosphere of fulfilment rather than resignation. The bird life is quiet, the surrounding countryside is still. Hidden in clusters of trees are the remote farmsteads and, standing like lighthouses, are the famous Marshland churches.

Churches are important features in the fens whether they have towers or spires, for they are often the only vertical in an otherwise horizontal landscape. And the churches in Marshland are among some of the most remarkable, not only in Britain, but in Europe.

At one time, in the late Saxon era, East Anglia was the wealthiest part of the country, and had thousands of churches. By the end of the eleventh century this area alone had a total of 1,400 churches standing, and although many have naturally disappeared some still remain—either altered or in ruins, but as clear evidence of the region's previous prosperity and importance. Many of these early churches were themselves built on earlier and often pre-Christian sites; some on pagan burial mounds, such as Maxey near Stamford, where remains of pagan cremations have been found, or at Ellough near Beccles.

Whatever discoveries we make about the past, it seems that there is always some earlier secret hidden beneath the stones or beneath the soil. Like the skeleton of the Bronze Age girl, life has been here longer than we care to think. So much must have been lost, buried or destroyed by our ancestors that we shall never know the full story. We only feel their presence as we walk quietly over their shadows.

The Marshland churches have a quality of their own whether you choose West Walton, Walpole St Peter, Terrington St Clement, or those buildings on the edge of the marshes at Holbeach and Long Sutton. The miracle is that so many of them are still standing, for over the centuries they have been subjected to some of the most violent floods this country has known. Most of them are built on land reclaimed from the sea and ever since they were built they have only been protected from the sea by the ancient Roman Bank. On many occasions that protection has not been enough and the villagers have fled to safety in the strong towers of the churches.

At West Walton some of this history is recorded on an ageing notice that expresses the people's praise to the Almighty God that:

saveth his people in all adversities be it kept in perpetual memory that on the first day of November 1613 the sea broke in and overflowed all Marshland to the great danger of men's lives and loss of goods. On the three and 20th Day of March 1614 this country was overflowed and on the 12th and 13th September 1670 all Marshland was again overflowed by the violence of the sea.

The churches have suffered many times from the sea's determination since the seventeenth century. Many times the bank has given way and the land has returned to the waters. As recently as 1947 the floods poured inland again as far as Crowland, and the abbey's Danger Bell was rung for the first time since 1880. And still the floods return and threaten, even though millions of pounds have been spent to prevent similar disasters.

Today, the marshes offer a spacious and ancient silence that makes me shiver with wonder rather than cold. More than anything else in nature it is what I search for and respect. Today, I am also lucky because no aircraft are about, zooming low over the Wash on practice bombing runs—a futile waste of money and energy I would have thought, as well as an insult to the silence. Some visits to the marshes can be ruined by those black, menacing machines racing and roaring down out of the clouds, diving and screaming over the mud-flats in a fantasy of destruction.

We are told that even the most sophisticated plane is virtually obsolete by the time it is brought into service and if conventional warfare is a thing of the past then I don't feel we are running too much risk to have the skies quiet for a day or so. But today they are absent from the sky, and the peace is undisturbed by thoughts of war or the bursting of invisible bombs.

I have come now to where the River Nene flows into the Wash. The old white lighthouse at Guy's Head glistens like a pillar of salt in the sun's brightness. Gulls enjoy the stillness of the air to indulge in a few acrobatics of their own. The atmosphere of this land between farm and sea is very real today, very intoxicating and lung-expanding.

The three main fenland rivers are not among the country's most attractive stretches of water, especially as they reach the lower land of their journey. The Great Ouse has the most interest as it makes its way from Downham Market to Denver Sluice and then on to its grand exit at King's Lynn. The Welland has a reasonably good flow through the Deepings, the outskirts of Crowland and the tree-lined banks of Spalding before its modest leave-taking at Fosdyke. But the Nene, once it leaves Northamptonshire, has some dull miles to cover between muddy banks and black fields before it slinks off, almost anonymously, to its outfall and the shallows of the Wash. Its last few miles are redeemed only by the North Brink at Wisbech—that lovely row of Georgian houses which gives the waterfront its individual quality and appeal. On a clear day when the houses are reflected in the water, when the paintwork shines and the creeper-leaves are changing colour, there is not a more attractive aspect to be found in any fenland town. The perspective and design, the dignity and character of those buildings by the Nene, help to brighten the river's last few miles.

But having said that I have to admit that I like the Nene and its dull monotony. I like its unfussy character and straightness. It has all the qualities of a fenman. And, like a fenman, it's not always as dull as it looks. Today it even flows with a degree of ageing majesty—a King Lear retiring greyly from the scenes and remnants of a divided kingdom.

Standing here at the land's edge it is not unlike being in some strange and almost mythical domain. The lungs inhale and exhale more deeply. The fresh air penetrates into every fibre. The eyes, lips, cheeks, hands, all feel different. The silence works through the mind, dispersing clinging worries like dandelion seeds blown from their stalk. You feel yourself more alive, more aware. Suddenly every nerve and cell is responding again to the power of the landscape, to its magic and challenge. It's like entering a theatre, you have to dispense with belief and let the unreality of the occasion lure you into a new reality, a new experience.

More than anything in nature I search for silence. Beautiful lakes lose their appeal once their tranquillity is disturbed and hills lose their strength once their calm is broken. The fen landscape can offer silence as well as solitariness though too often its companion is the west wind and its bullying can spoil what would otherwise be tranquil.

But today there is no wind, and there is no noise in the sky or on the land. Here where all the roads end, here at the edge of place where neither sea nor land will give into each other, I have found silence.

I sit on a bank of yellow grass surrounded by immense distances. Before me the mud-flats of the Wash and on the horizon a glint of the sea. Behind me the silt fens and lonely farms of Lincolnshire to the north, and the subtle changing land of Norfolk to the south.

There is nothing we can do with silence: we cannot commercialize it or exploit it, because for most of us it is useless. But it can do things to us: it can prove its unique sovereignty in a way nothing else can. Silence is absolute, contained within itself and older than anything known to us. Time itself was a seed sown in silence and grew out of silence. We cannot measure it. We cannot see it. It is more intangible than the wind, more powerful than the sea. We cannot touch it. Yet we can *feel* it. It can overpower us sometimes with its antiquity. It saw the formation of the first clouds and gave voice to thunder and fire. Everything that has sound grew out of the silence. And silence will be there when there is no more sound. Music and language would be a monotony of noise without silence, and it is a condition already willingly chosen by a large mass of modern civilization afraid of being left naked and unprotected before the eyes of silence.

I am lucky today for I have found a deep, healing silence under a vast sky now streaked with thin layers of motionless cloud. Far off I can see patterns of flight as birds weave movement into the silence. If I shouted into the air there would be no echo. You cannot break the silence here as easily as you can in mountain country. There the silence has rocks that can reject your shouts, that can throw back your words as irrelevant things. Words belong to man, not to mountains. Out here you would certainly not have your protests even returned. The syllables would be immediately swallowed up in the great "nothingness" we cannot harness, bottle, utilize or sell. The sky today is a deep reserve of silence, a giant predator that could suck in all the stars and planets that are known to us.

Is that why we are afraid? Why we defend ourselves with a vast armoury of noise? Is that why we hurry from its penetrating and devouring stare?

But today there is no menace, no threat, no fear, only the prolonged satisfaction of feeling the rhythm of the earth moving again slowly between two points in Time. And the grass is a million years old. The thread of water on the horizon slowly broadens towards the land, a roll of silk on a loom of mud. And the sun has pushed this roundabout round a little more. And I find myself straining now to listen to the farthest and most inaudible echo of the silence somewhere beyond this earth's beginning. The degree of happiness I feel cannot be measured or compared with any other kind of happiness. And I know that I've been lucky today.

I don't want to move or go home but for my own safety I must be off these marshes before evening comes in. There is no joy being lost out here on this no-man's-land with high tide coming arm-in-arm with the darkness and mist. I have sat for over three hours letting the afternoon soak through my skin and into the bones and I feel as if I have been away from the towns for more than a year.

Even the small towns of the fens come as a shock when you return to them—Holbeach, Terrington, Wisbech, the busy A47, the heavy lorries, the home-going traffic, the rush and noise of overtaking vehicles, the queues at traffic-lights, the congested city with its concentration of noise and smells. It all seems so alien and the body has about one hour to re-orientate itself after being in that period of Time for which we have no measurement.

Having done some work but wanting still more of the day, or rather the night, I go out again to the edge of town and get caught up in a new excitement and wonder as I look up at the sky.

> Wanting nothing more than the dark fields
> and cool air drifting in unhindered from the Wash,
> I feel twice blessed to find above the fens
> this half-forgotten miracle of sky—

visible blackness glistening with stars
and breath of bats' wings haunting willow trees.

> Beyond the fields a copper-coloured moon
> stipples the waters of the River Nene,
> flecking the shadows with the flight of moths.
> I would have been content with only these,

but suddenly above the quiet grass
I find this other country and forget the earth.

So many blessings in one day. It is nearly two o'clock and I can hear the wind blowing through the trees, giving life to the darkness.

Nearer the Sea

A different area of marshland with the same quality of silence and solitariness is found beyond the fens in north Norfolk; especially where the salt-marshes around Thornham, Brancaster, Blakeney and Overy Staithe create their own mystery out of the sky and water.

There are different kinds of silence. The silence of an empty room, or a church, or a theatre when the play has ended, is full of the characters and the people it has known; such a silence can haunt, even oppress. Then there is the silence of a field early in the morning, or by a river-bank, or on a hillside; a shallow silence which creates a pleasant response in us of restfulness and comfort. Then there is the silence of a mountain-top, or the saltmarshes. This silence can be awesome and hypnotic, spell-binding and challenging. It is a deep silence that we know would be there whether man existed or not.

I first discovered this quality in the Norfolk saltmarshes several years ago when I was walking along the beach from Old Hunstanton to Brancaster. It was farther than I expected and when I came to a sea wall I made my way inland to find, perhaps, a pub and then a lift on the main road back to Hunstanton.

The path from the sand-dunes brought me into the village of Thornham and to the old white-washed inn that looks out towards the sea. There I was able to enjoy a good pint of beer drawn from the wood, a small warm loaf and some cheese, as well as a long rest from the mid-day sun and my ambitious walk.

It is a place to which I have returned many times and it is a landscape that never fails to reward. The rough tracks down to the creek and the walk towards the sea have an atmosphere that is quite unlike anything else I know, especially in the evenings. The rich light of the setting sun gives a golden shimmer to the reeds and grass and deepens the red of the roof-tiles on a nearby boathouse. Gulls and oyster-catchers electrify the stillness with their anxious cries which echo for a few moments and then dissolve in the silence. Far-off the sea begins its return to high-tide. The water in the creek ripples. The air is timeless and unpolluted. It could have been like this five hundred years ago. It may still be like it in five hundred years to come.

I have sometimes taken friends out there, people with whom I wanted to share this experience, people from quite different landscapes. I remember once taking a friend from Bristol, a man who had known nothing but city life and had no love of the countryside. The fens had certainly not converted him, but standing one evening on Thornham marshes he turned to me and said, 'This is it, this is what I've been wanting to find . . . now I know what you're always talking about.' The golden light, the thin cries of the birds, the smell of salt, the inaudible movements of reeds, the special "spirit of place" filled us with pleasure and contentment. It was an experience that was shared and unforgettable.

A few miles farther along the coast is Overy Staithe and here the marshes gain in scope and impressiveness. The maze of muddy creeks and samphire beds, the greater variety of birds and acres of marsh, the quickly changing tides and low winds can be even more terrifying, but they can also be more warm and accommodating, more hospitable and intimate. I would not want them always, or for too long. I am a man of the earth rather than of the sea. But they give that marvellous feeling of detachment and freedom from the present. They may not, in the end, be for me as wholly satisfying as a landscape of rich fields, never as productive as the farms, never as changing and unpredictable as the fens. Even so, I like to be out as far as I can get on the marshes at some time during the year so that I feel I have had the best of both worlds.

On a few occasions I have been lucky enough to stay at the Tower Mill, an experience that enriches one's understanding of these wild tracts of land and water, especially at night time. Although you cannot see the water you know it is out there. From one of the high windows, when the sky is moon-lit, you can just see the shadowy marshes and the glint of winding creeks. It's like being becalmed in a five-storey ark, waiting for the flood of darkness to recede or for some strange wind to blow you gently out to sea. The solid walls groan but never give way. The white sails bend but never break.

I have been at the Mill in spring when the long hours of daylight have allowed us to sit out of doors for supper and walks have been possible along the sea-wall without the fear of getting lost. And I have been in late autumn when the Norfolk lanes have been blessed with all the colours of October and the darkness has closed in upon us at five o'clock so that the long evening could be spent around the fire, talking and reading to each other until midnight.

To come back to that Mill after a day out on the marshes is one of those simple pleasures that we do not easily forget. The white-washed walls, the wooden furniture, the smell of supper and the colour of a glass of whisky by candlelight make previous concepts of luxury crumble. After a meal of poached eggs, cooked samphire (that we had picked ourselves that day) and home-made bread, we gather round a table of warmth, of oil-lamps and steaming soup. Then we climb up one flight of steps to the next room with its low beams, its rows of books, its glowing fire and small windows looking out on the night and there, our bodies still glowing with the day's walking and the meal, we relax. Outside the wind is blowing, the night is very still. The mill absorbs the silence and weaves us into its spell. We speak quietly, read and listen quietly. You can almost feel the Mill rocking.

After a day exposed to the wild influences
of Norfolk saltmarshes, where terns and oyster-catchers
have seldom been silent about our intrusion,
we have come home to the tar-weathered walls
of this towering windmill.

Above us the sails are fixed in silence.
Mist anchors our ark to a sea-bed of barley
as we gather round a table of bright words.
Pale flames cast shadows on the floor, and smoke
winds round the low white beams.

Now there's a calm no violence can break,
a peace that penetrates the bones.
Beyond the fields the moon lies stranded in a creek
and those protesting birds at last are still.
Then, fading the bloom of oil-lamps into night,
we let our bodies drift into the depths of sleep.

On other nights the hours have not been so calm and I have been a guest there when gales have blown down trees in the fields and washed boats up on to the main road, when rain has slashed at the sails and light-ning struck at the walls. But although chaos was let loose in the lanes and creeks the mill stood firm, the ark sheltered us all and kept us safe.

Choosing Roads

There are several ways to travel from the fenlands to Norfolk's marshland. The main routes, either from Wisbech to King's Lynn, or from Downham Market to Swaffham and Fakenham, take you on busy roads that get you there quickly; but there are other roads—lonely, winding roads that lead you through a maze of hedgerows and fields before you emerge on to high ground overlooking the sea.

I always prefer to choose roads that take me through a variety of landscapes—from the low black fens between Outwell and Runcton to the greener contours of West Acre and Massingham, and then through the Birchams or South Creake, to Burnham Market and the coast. Ruined priories, forgotten abbeys, historic houses and castles, ancient hedges and unusual churches prolong, rather than delay, the journey. Flint cottages and village greens at well-spaced intervals give to the landscape a generous feeling of leisure and plenty, so that when your destination is reached it is a fulfilment rather than an achievement.

I don't like ancient ruins of any kind to be *too* well cared-for or laid out with immaculate lawns and "Keep off the grass" notices, suggesting a corpse lying in state. The regulations and systems of modern bureaucracy frighten the old ghosts away, and leave the place with only the reminders of yesterday's visitors. Ruins need a few clusters of nettles and some dusty corners, a bit of creeper on the walls and some uneven paths. Well-cut borders and gravelled aisles destroy the atmosphere, take away the original footprints and dilute the spirit of the past.

Protect the ruins, yes. Make them as uniform as Odeon cinemas, no. More and more, I feel, the remoteness and individuality of our abbeys, priories and castles, is being spoilt by an over-enthusiastic "white-collar philosophy" that sees these genuine remnants of the eleventh century as suitable settings for plastic gnomes, gift-shops and civic illuminations, or their equivalent.

Norfolk was once free from this modern mania, but Progress is catching up. The ghosts and ruins of the old Cluniac Order are giving in, or rather are having to make way for the new orders from Whitehall, even at such a quiet and isolated place as Castle Acre. Will there soon be no stones left where we can feel the grandeur of a lost age without today's "survival kits"—cardboard tea-cups, plastic bags and coloured postcards?

E

The answer for the solitary seeker is, as always, to go out of season if you can, or after closing-time when no one is looking; otherwise seek for the peace you want in those untravelled byways that can still be found, especially in this benign county.

Times change so quickly and the hunger for the countryside is so great that I hardly dare breathe the names of places where peace has so far been preserved. One fears too much the invasion of crowds not wanting solitude but just somewhere different to congregate for the week-end ritual of comparing cars, caravans, tents and tea-pots; somewhere different to read the Sunday newspapers or listen to those endless radio programmes that always sound worse out in the country.

I believe it is vitally important to preserve what wildness there is in this diminishing countryside of ours. Animals, plants and birds also have a place on this earth, and there are thousands of young people growing up who do want to be quiet, who do want to know the wildness and freedom from cities. We must keep in mind the often expressed feeling of Henry David Thoreau:

We need the tonic of wildness. . . . In wildness is the preservation of the world.

That necessary wildness is being bullied into the corner, is being pushed out of our lives. Although nature is often quick to recover, it is not very good at protecting itself. And it is while we're here that we want the wildness of nature, not when it's too late.

For a less winding and solitary journey into north Norfolk there is always the main route through King's Lynn, and the opportunity of slipping out from the busy traffic into the old town itself.

Lynn is indeed a favourite town of mine; a town of music, markets, shops, docks, churches and old buildings that become a world within a world. The atmosphere of the place quickly tones up the tired limbs and sharpens the mind: the air is bright and clear with a tang of salt at the edges. It is always benevolent. It takes you in with a welcome as old as its history. Every corner says, "Look, have you seen me? And me? And me?"

So far Lynn has managed to retain much of its ancient appeal, absorbing the growth of modern industry and the growing traffic at the docks without panic or loss of grace. It has made room for pedestrians as well as motorists. It has accommodated art as well as commerce. It is at one and the same time the gateway to the sea and the gateway to the fens. It has been so for five or six thousand years, though its monopoly on this side of the Wash covers little more than one thousand years. It has known the battle for survival against the most fiercesome neighbour it could have had—water. It has known the ravages of man and the struggles of Civil War. As early as the fourteenth century Lynn was established in an important position in the English economy: in 1347 the town contributed nineteen ships to Edward III's expeditionary fleet against France, while London provided only five more. It was then the third largest port in England and continued to thrive despite growing competition from ports in the south and west. In 1722 Daniel Defoe visited Lynn and wrote that it was "a rich and populous thriving port . . . supplying six counties wholly and three counties in part with their goods, especially wines and coals". Now it sends out goods from Britain to the Common Market and beyond and returns supplies to every part of the country. It's importance has grown even more in the last two or three years. And yet, once, it had to fight for its trade with what is now a harmless village a few miles away —Castle Rising.

I shall be returning to Castle Rising later in the year. I won't distract now from the achievements of King's Lynn for at almost every turn you realize that you are surrounded by evidence of its success and history, not only in the churches, the Town Hall and many old buildings, but also in the alley-ways and court-yards, the cobbled lanes and timbered houses.

My own favourite corner of King's Lynn is between St Margaret's Church and Hampton Court, and especially St Margaret's Lane that takes you not only down to the South Quay but also back to the fifteenth century. There the impressive row of Warehouses, that were once the seat of the Hanseatic League, immediately cast their spell and lure the imagination back into a life five hundred years ago. Hampton Court, Trinity Guildhall and Clifton House are obvious attractions, but there are many more fascinating reminders of the town's past carved modestly on doorposts or in the bricks, on roof-rafters or gable-ends. It is still a very human town, where past and present meet almost every human need, where "evocations in the air" blow away the dates on calendars and make the written history books poor substitutes.

On one hand, then, the gateway to north Norfolk and the lonely beaches and marshes; on the other the gateway back to the fens and the low black fields. My choice this time has to be back home to fen country.

A Different Childhood

Thurlby is a small village of Scandinavian origin, a village on the western boundary of the fens between Market Deeping and Bourne. Its name means "Thurulf's village" and comes from those days when this part of Lincolnshire knew many Danish settlements after the invasion of 876.

It's a good piece of country with the lowlands on one side and the land rising noticeably on the other with a greater abundance of trees and more cattle in the fields.

Tonight the sun loitered for a few moments on the horizon, allowing a layer of streaky clouds to turn crimson for five minutes and then the colour drained from the sky and it was dusk.

I'd had tea with some friends at New Farm, where a parting gift of newly-dug potatoes reminded me again of what a lovely smell they give with the damp soil still on them. Then I made my way back to the village to talk with Mrs Harris about her own childhood in the fens.

We sat before an open fire where the coal burned cosily. Her dog slept on the hearth-rug. The heavy curtains shut out the darkness of the night. It was a quiet night, country-quiet and unhurried.

Into that warm, comfortable stillness came the memories of a childhood that was lived before the First World War. The talk was filled with the characters and events that had become legendary through the generations that separated us.

You can hear the same stories of the fen-man's uncompromising attitude and independence wherever you meet with good fen talkers. Fenmen have always been fighters. They have had to be. They have fought their way through many catastrophes of floods, fires, epidemics, depressions, hungers, hardships and killing winters. They have not been called "fen-tigers" for nothing and their stubbornness is more than just cussedness. The land has made them what they are.

Mrs Harris reminded me that some of those winters could last long enough to starve families to death. 'There could be fourteen weeks of frost sometimes which meant no work on the land and no money coming in either.'

'What did people do for food then?' I asked.

Well, they would have salted some down ready for the winter and of course they could take part in the Bread and Meat Races to see if they could get something there.'

'You mean ice-skating?'

'That's right. As you know the Fenmen were the best skaters in the country and when the rivers and dykes were frozen you went everywhere on your skates, or "runners" as we used to call them. I could skate by the time I was four years old. It was almost as natural as walking to us in those days. I can remember when I first started skating my father would take all of us on to the ice, he would have a clothes prop which he would hold cross-ways in the middle, then we would line-up each side of him and off we'd go. After a couple of days of that you didn't need any clothes prop to hang on to any more, you could skate.'

'Tell me more about the Bread and Meat Races.'

'Well, they'd be held all over the fens. I can remember the races that used to be held from Ramsey to Pondersbridge and from Ramsey to Chatteris, and even from Whittlesey to Peterborough. Then, as you know, there were always the big meetings on the flooded washlands near the Dog-in-a-Doublet. If you were a good skater you could win a leg of mutton or a pig's head, some bacon and a loaf or two of bread. But mind you, you had to be good, because men came from all over to take part. Some men kept their families alive throughout the winter from what they won at skating. You made yourself as good as possible, not just for fun but for survival.'

I remembered some of those skating scenes from my own childhood when the floodwater used to reach the edge of town and hundreds of acres would become one huge sheet of ice. The ice would be crowded with men and children. It was a very Dutch scene, a scene that cannot easily be imagined or re-created today on the smaller areas of ice. The old skating days were much more expansive. I can't remember any Bread and Meat Races as such, but I know that my grandfather used to help sweep the courses for a few pence or take a chair on his back which he would hire out to the gentry who wanted to sit down to fix their skates, or 'pattens'. Some would have an area specially roped off for themselves so that they could indulge in a bit of figure-skating before a hungry audience. Trades-men used to do a brisk business there too.

'I suppose Antonio the chestnut man was before your time, wasn't he?' asked Mrs Harris.

'Yes, in my day it was Tom Blake with his fish-and-chip van and he'd serve you with a generous bag of hot chips for a penny.'

We spoke about the competition that always went on in the villages, not only for food but for the skates themselves. There was always an argument as to whether "Whittlesey Runners" were better than "Ramsey Runners" and it depended, of course, on where you lived. When the Norwegian skates were introduced into the fens the local makes were quickly forgotten and a few of the old customs disappeared too. But there are still a few pairs of "Whittlesey Runners" rusting away in a few sheds and garages I know. Although the original wearers have long since ceased to use skates, their sons have kept them for the memories they evoke.

Our conversation turned from skaters to blacksmiths and Mrs Harris's grandfather, who was a well-known smithy in the area. In those days one of his jobs was to go round the farms "paring" yearlings to strengthen their hooves for the soft fenland soil, which would have allowed the young hoof to spread, and also to prepare the horses for shoeing when they were two-year-olds.

'When you got a job then you hung on to it and a lot of the boys would have to leave home to live on the job or with the master to whom they were apprenticed. It was expected of them, when you had a family of ten or eleven you couldn't keep 'em all at home, especially if they were mixed and you only had two bedrooms. So when a boy left school it meant that he also had to pack his box and go off to live with whoever hired him or took him on. If a boy was lucky he could get taken on at a farm for £3 a year plus his keep. But mind you, he had to stay for at least a year otherwise he didn't get a penny. Hiring time was at Whittlesey Statutes Fair and it's common sense that the strong ones were snapped up first. If a mother was able to write a line at all to her son, she always ended with this prayer, "I hope that God is with you and that you'll have a good winter's work".'

'What about the girls, I suppose they went into domestic service?'

'Yes, and they had to be just as careful. Their honesty was tested more than once.'

'How do you mean?'

'Well, the mistress would put a gold sovereign under the carpet or under the sideboard runner to see whether the girl would dust there in the first place and then pocket what she found. If she didn't move it she'd be accused of not doing her job properly and if she did touch it she'd be accused of intending to steal. Either way she was made to feel that she was being watched even when there was no one in the room. But I knew one girl who found a sovereign under the carpet in the house where she worked and she made no bones about it. She picked it up, took it to her mistress and said, "This must be your'n, ma'am, but if I find another one under the carpet next time then it'll be mine." That's how independent they could be, even though it meant risking their job.'

The hours went too quickly. We talked of country cures, of harvests, chapels, Sunday School Outings and many of the traditions that have disappeared since World War Two as well as those lost after World War One. Mrs Harris returns quite often to the heart of her native fens and shares with me the great influence and power they have to draw their own back to them.

'I can't get them out of my system,' she said, 'even after all these years. A little while ago I was up in the Lake District and went to the Grasmere Sports and, d'you know, within minutes I was cheering so wildly that I thought I was back at Coates' Sports day sixty years ago, and you know as well as I do that there's not much in Coates to remind you of Grasmere.'

At the end of it all I left with her last sentences ringing clearly and unforgettably in my head. 'I can think of no greater joy,' she said, 'than to nestle down by a haystack and look at that great wide, open, free landscape. It has such immensity, such cleanness. To me the fen country is like a big mother, it's so dear, so understanding. It relieves sorrow and takes you back with such generosity. You might think I'm a bit sentimental about it when I say that for me it's a spiritual experience. It's like going into a huge cathedral. I don't find the fens lonely, like you perhaps do, but I think I understand what you are trying to say when you talk about their solitude . . . but why are we trying to explain? We *know* what they mean to us, don't we!'

We stood at the front door of her house and I was immediately impressed by the stillness of the night, the country-stillness. There was not a sound. Above me the stars shone brightly in a dark sky not discoloured by the neon-signs of a city. There was the sweet smell of autumn in the air, a fen sweetness of rising mist, of earth and sky. Yes, we *knew* and did not have to explain.

The midnight roads were empty and my drive home was in a haze of memory and gratitude. I could not bother to put the car away. I went into the garden and looked up again to the stars and breathed in the cool air. Far off a church clock chimed some quarter between the hours and I knew it was already morning.

A Resting Day

When I was having my breakfast this morning the first autumn blue-tit arrived in the garden and had a quick look at the bird-box and the empty nut-basket. That's another little job that must be done now, another preparation for winter. Slowly, all the familiar signs and reminders are coming along as one season prepares the way for another. Leaves are beginning to change colour quite quickly now and soon October will reach the climax of its pageantry.

There are some days when I want to write and the words are nowhere to be found, when even the generous landscape fails to inspire something. Then the frustration sets in and the typewriter stares back with hostile mockery. Nothing goes right. The keys stick. The pen runs out of ink. Even the filing of accumulated letters provokes a temper.

When your livelihood is writing then a non-productive day like this is worse than taking a day off for a funeral. It's like waiting in the rain for a train or a bus that never comes. I get impatient and blame myself.

But the other day a saner and wiser person said to me, 'You can't expect every day to give you something, surely?'

I said, 'But why not? I go to bed each night full of expectancy for the morning and all that the new day has to offer. There must be something.'

'And you do that seven days a week?'

'Well, yes. I have to.'

'Then you're very foolish. Don't you realize that the days must also be given a rest. It's like asking a field to give seven harvests a year, year after year. You can't keep taking all the time. You must learn to give some days a rest. You must learn to be still, or at least to do something else.'

So today I have sawn the branches we have collected into logs ready for the winter fires and have chopped several boxes of kindling which I have now stacked in the garage. And I have learnt again how good a change is and how lovely the smell of wood is as it splits, letting fifty or more summers rise from the white wounds. The different smells, the different textures, the sticky sap or the clean dry slice, all appeal to the senses. And all these summers will go towards our fires. My father was once a carpenter and knows the smell and grain of wood enough to give each log an identity. . . . "That's elm . . . that's sycamore."

It's been a good, physically tiring day. After supper I even deny myself

a book and instead listen to the music of a man as English as an oak tree—
Edward Elgar. Here was a man who, surely, drew from his landscape as
much as anyone. It is music of the open-air and the English countryside,
but it is also music that comes out of a man's love of that countryside. It
doesn't always have to be the hill-striding music of his more exuberant
pieces. Even the slow Elegy for Strings has the right kind of autumnal
melancholy to end this resting day and brings with it the smell of wood,
of fallen leaves, of night.

Harvest Festivals

I looked in vain this morning for a swallow or housemartin, but they have
all gone I think, and the telegraph wires are empty for another year.

The harvest is finished too after several set-backs and struggles. Those
who were able to cut early had indeed been lucky. Those who'd had to
wait because of breaks in the weather eventually had more than just the
rain to contend with. Unusually strong winds for the time of year beat
the crops and in many fields blew the grain out of the ears.

But lucky or unlucky, the men have won and the harvests have been
gathered. Bales of straw still stand in some fields waiting to be collected.
In the morning mist and uncertain light they might be mistaken for druid
stones, and although the fens may never have known druids, these grey
shapes are enough to let the imagination hear strange chanting and pagan
incantations in the air. There must be some spirit of thanksgiving for
harvest in the fens, apart from the annual chapel harvest festivals. Perhaps
this is one reason why harvest festival services are still so popular.

The non-conformist movement had plenty of support at one time in the
fens. There are not many hamlets that do not have a Baptist, Methodist
or Zion chapel still standing and in use. At home we had two churches,
six chapels, the Salvation Army and a Mission Hall, which wasn't bad for
a population then of less than 8,000, especially when the devil had
fifty-two pubs to offer as an alternative. In some of the small towns the
congregations made no secret of competing with each other for the
best harvest festival and would go to them all to compare.

Harvest festivals were always an attraction, like the Sunday School
Outings. We prepared for the Harvest Weekend during several weeks
before it arrived. Vegetables were coaxed towards perfection. Flowers
were protected by butterfly nets. Only the best of what we had grown was

good enough to take to chapel. Eggs were chosen with care and sacrifice. Potatoes were scrubbed clean. Parsnips were washed to a creamy yellow and the apples polished until they shone. Marrows and pumpkins were always something of a novelty for they had often been engraved with a text or line from a hymn in their early days of growth, so that by the time the marrow or pumpkin was ready for cutting the letters stood out clear and bold on their hard skin. By the time we staggered with them to the chapel it was like carrying the Commandment tablets inscribed by Moses himself.

Sheaves of corn were given by farmers. A harvest loaf was baked and presented by one of the town's bakers, and even a sack of coal was given by one of the coalmen. There were exotic gifts like peaches and pomegranates burning like braziers. There were bunches of grapes and baskets of oranges, boxes of nuts, packets of figs and hands of bananas. To walk into chapel on Harvest Sunday was like falling into the hold of a ship just back from the distant tropics. For children not used to seeing such abundance it was like being taken to a pantomine or shown into Aladdin's cave. Flowers hid the pulpit, and often the preacher. We had a choir of dahlias and pillars of chrysanthemums. There was a sweet smell of apples and a tangy whiff of celery. The choir-master always told us that there was a fieldmouse still hiding in one of the sheaves of corn, a tame threat to prevent us from stripping the ears and rubbing them in our hands to find the sweet kernels for eating. There was so much of everything that we wondered how it would ever get sold or eaten. No wonder we sang with considerable gusto:

> Come, ye thankful people, come,
> Raise the song of harvest home,
> All is safely gathered in
> Ere the winter storms begin . . .

For the children the greatest fun of the Harvest Festival was in fact the sale of produce on the Monday evening. Everything was carried into the schoolroom and then auctioned off by a member of the chapel who was very skilled at making you pay twice as much as you would have been charged for the same item in the local shops. He could even persuade you to buy back something that you had taken. But as it was all in aid of the chapel fund no one seemed to mind what they paid. I usually came away from the sale with my annual coconut, pomegranate, bag of monkey-nuts and a stolen apple bulging in my trouser pocket. Once my father bought the harvest loaf, which was the shape and size of a real sheaf of corn, and my sister and I broke pieces off as we walked home and ate them, crisp, tasty and wholesome without any butter.

With the end of the Harvest Festival, summer was really over and the days were sandwiched more and more between misty mornings and darkening afternoons. There was something about autumn that I didn't understand. It had this strange calming effect on the town. Days grew quieter as well as shorter. The people too relaxed into a moodiness that changed their personalities. Some houses were almost like tortoises and seemed to hibernate for winter. We never saw the people who lived in them. The amber sunlight shone on their old walls during the late autumn days and the snow stayed unswept outside their doors until it melted. Then spring came and the front door opened again and we saw the people emerge.

I was reminded of these simple joys last year when I was taking a coach-load of people on a Sunday afternoon tour of the fens. It was in the autumn and we were travelling the narrow road along Ten Mile Bank towards Denver Sluice. Twilight was already gaining too quickly upon us and I was anxious to get to Denver while there was still some light left for us to appreciate that impressive piece of engineering that controls the waters of the Great Ouse. But a few miles before we reached the sluice we found our way blocked by a car parked outside the small church. The service had already started and we had to assume that the car owner was in the congregation. Beyond the building the last stubble-fires were still burning on Hilgay Fen and as we sat there wondering what to do the strains of the hymn reached us—"Come, ye thankful people, come . . ."

We were not feeling particularly thankful at that moment as the darkness gathered in and Denver now looked out of the question. But the sound of singing took my mind back to those days when it meant something to be part of a simple faith and community, and the feeling of being excluded from these villagers' joys and thanksgiving was intensified by our helplessness on an expensive coach that could not move until they had finished raising their harvest home. One or two people in the coach even started to join in the singing and, somehow, Denver Sluice didn't matter then. We drove home in the dark and let the memories of the afternoon— Holme Fen, Wicken Fen, Ely and Littleport—mix with those memories brought back by our unexpected delay on Ten Mile Bank.

Sky and Water

After three days and nights of rain a new morning wakens me to a brightness that is dazzling and fresh. The sky is stretched tight like a blue balloon, its skin so taut, so translucent, that if a bird could fly high enough and touch it with its beak it would burst, revealing all the great secrets beyond, or the great nothing.

But no bird can fly that high for these transparent walls of the sky today look so very high, so far away, that no pin-prick from this earth can harm them.

It is a day on which you can see the space exaggerated by the clouds. Some days clouds look as if they are sewn on to the sky like grey patches. Some days the clouds are the sky and the height of the sky is no higher than the clouds. But today the clouds are so detached from that unreachable sky that you can see the great distances beyond.

It's a three-dimensional day—rooftops, clouds, sky; all separated by immense space. And the spaces shine with a brilliance that is crystalline. The light that floods over the earth gives a sharpness even to buildings on the horizon. Windows of farmhouses glisten. White buildings shine like icebergs. And whitest of all are the wings of a swan as it flies over the fields, its wings and its long straight neck, whiter than snow.

The movement of the clouds emphasize the stillness of the space beyond. The blue is permanent, the white convoys are transitory. Today the wind has so much room in which to run wild. It is almost delirious in its freedom and blows in all directions. The weather vanes are not still for a second. They turn, spin, swivel and grow dizzy with the wind's behaviour.

It is a day for being outdoors, away from streets and houses, a day for enjoying the pleasure of movement after the rain's prison. Suddenly all the iron bars are taken away. The locks have been turned.

The roads are empty. The fields are deserted. I walk by the side of a dyke and see the sky reflected in water. Here are two of the most important elements of the fen country—water and sky. Without either this landscape would not be the same, it would indeed be a dull prison always.

The sheltered water in the dyke is still. I watch the reflection of the reeds swaying beneath the surface. Deeper down are the clouds floating through the dark brown water. The stillness is broken by a moorhen chugging from one bank to the other. Then the reflections return as the ripples melt into the black peaty soil.

I leave the course of the dyke and make my away along Hod Fen towards Holme Fen Nature Reserve. The vulnerability of this landscape to strong westerly winds is shown again in the rows of telegraph poles leaning at precarious angles along the road. This is an area of land, between Yaxley and Ramsey, where in springtime you will most likely see a fen-blow, one of those terrifying dust-storms that can plane the top-soil off the fields and blow it in great rolling clouds for several miles. This is land where you will see heaps of bog-oaks piled up at the edge of a field after ploughing—black torsos of trees buried for 6,000 years or more in the peat and now revealed again as the level of peat dwindles to just a few feet.

This, too, is where you can see the famous Holme Fen Post that has recorded the erosion and shrinkage of the land over the last hundred and twenty years. The top of that post is now fourteen and a half feet above ground level. In 1851 it was buried vertically into the soil until only the cap could be seen. This is the land that was once on the edge of Whittlesey Mere, the last stretch of inland water to be drained from the fens in the nineteenth century. It is an area where you can feel nearly all the essential qualities of a fen landscape—water, sky, reeds, marsh-plants, wild-fowl and rich farmland.

Holme Fen Nature Reserve is a wild paradise of plants, trees, mosses and ferns. The most common tree is the birch—surviving in such numbers from the end of the nineteenth century when hundreds of trees were planted to provide game coverts. In narrow glades or at a turn in the path you will see a row of alder, an isolated pine or a solitary sycamore, even a high bush of rhododendron. After a wet spell the black peaty soil of the paths makes them like interior sprung mattresses and you almost bounce along between banks of bramble, bracken and moss.

Today is such a day and the smell of the undergrowth is sweet and ancient. A protected cushion of moss is more like a galaxy of green stars. The rosebay willow herb (or Fireweed, as the Americans call it) has finished flowering and the feathery seeds swirl into the air like white smoke from a bonfire or a cloud of gnats caught in the golden rays of the sun. A robin sings on a fallen branch. Above the tree-tops the sky is a vivid blue beyond the silver bark of the birches. The stillness closes around you. It is a different kind of silence from what you will feel out in the open spaces. The silence of woods is more intimate and very close. It comes to you. The silence of fields is powerful and far-reaching. It draws you on.

Leaving the woods and walking again on the open road between the two sides of the Reserve I stop to look at the variety of reeds and sedge lining the dykeside. They sway gently like a silent metronome. Their sage-green leaves and silken heads catch the light. The water is as brown as old beer. The grass is long and wet. Blackberries are ripening in juicy clusters. Hips hang bright and tempting like miniature Chianti bottles full of light red wine. Pheasants strut in a nearby field and a crop of carrots waits to be lifted, their bright green tops as tall as ferns. When they are pulled out of such soot-blackness their orange roots glow. I was given one to taste and it snapped with a sweetness and tang as rich as the soil. It seemed criminal to put such natural flavour into cans, to take that raw quality away from it and substitute chemicals. Why do we have to take the taste of the earth away from our root vegetables? Washed carrots, celery and potatoes that have sweated for a few days in a plastic bag after having all the soil washed from them cannot compare with those dug freshly for the pot.

From Holme Fen the day beckoned me on to Ramsey, but before leaving the edge of the Nature Reserve I had to stop again to look over what had been Whittlesey Mere and try to imagine once more the great regattas that used to be held there. It was difficult to see sailing boats and small launches, picnic parties and top-hatted gentlemen chasing butterflies. I even found it difficult to remember that the Northamptonshire poet, John Clare, used to walk all the way from Helpston to here to study rare ferns. Now only the silent fields and their crops existed where once the water had held plenty of fish and riches from Ramsey abbey.

Ramsey, like several of the 'islands' that stood in the Great Fen before drainage work started, had a wealthy abbey with fertile meadows and gardens. An ancient rhyme records that as "Thorney was the flower of many fair tree" so Ramsey was "rich of gold and fee". Today a spacious lawn is spread in front of the ruined gatehouse and, neighbouring it, is the parish church with a fine Norman nave, a colonade of pillars—of which no two are alike—and a small chancel of great calm.

A relative of Oliver Cromwell is believed to have brought the plague to Ramsey in 1666 by ordering some cloth from London. William Cromwell and his tailor were among the four hundred victims of the plague who were buried in the churchyard, a plague which, as Daniel Defoe records in his *Journal of the Plague Year*, also spread to Peterborough, Norwich, Colchester and Lincoln, aggravated possibly by people travelling from one city to another in an effort to ease the burden on their own houses or to escape into safer quarters.

Several roads lead from Ramsey to either Chatteris or Bury and the fens beyond. You can leave by the road that passes the village green and the pond or take the quiet road into Ramsey Hollow, where you get a very real feeling of the fen country. The fields are rich and black. The dykes are lined with reeds and sedge. The low level of this area of land in a low-lying landscape is quite dramatic. It is a hollow in every sense of the word. There is a hollow in the land, a hollow sound in the air, a ghostly feeling of silence as evening creeps in from the surrounding fields. I stopped the car again and stood at an open gate to look over a field that even had a slight elevation, the furrows rising towards the brow of the fens boundary. The thought of being caught out there on a foggy night was enough to make me leave quickly, for the road that led on to Ramsey Forty Foot, Ramsey Mereside and back home, is notorious for mist and fog that can deceive even the local people into taking a wrong turn. I have heard stories of ghosts too, ghosts of Scottish soldiers killed by the locals of 350 years ago when Vermuyden had to use imported labour to drain the fens and put some of the men on guard at nights, men who mysteriously disappeared until their ghosts returned to haunt the fields.

Not wanting to test my disbelief in ghosts or run the risk of getting caught in any mist, I drove home without any further stops until I came to the familiar streets of Whittlesey and the North Bank road that goes to Peterborough. Then I imagined all sorts of phantoms I might have seen.

Sunday

Church-going is not a regular habit of mine. I can't go week after week without question. I can't participate in all of the services or festivals that require a submission from me that I cannot give whole-heartedly. There are often doubts, often times when I feel that perhaps we are deceiving ourselves, that our rituals are no different from those pre-Christian religions that served the same purpose and demanded the same obedience.

But I can't dismiss these doubts as easily as that without realizing too that there are times when I do attend church and feel greatly enriched by the service, when I do feel lighter in spirit through having been part of something that has so far proved indestructible and has preserved in language and music some of the noblest ideas of western civilization as well as, for some, an unshakeable faith.

So some weeks I find myself a willing contributor to the hymn-singing and chanting and other weeks I find myself rebelling against what, for me becomes the empty monotony of it all. I know that living in this kind of spiritual no-man's-land exposes my own weakness more than that of any organized religion. The weekly running of a church, with its bazaars and social chit-chat, discourages me from being more actively employed in doing anything about it. My faith is a very hit and miss affair.

Having said that I also have to admit that there are times when I feel excluded from something very real, human and lasting. Common sense tells me it's wrong to expect perfection, that the reason why the Church only appeals to 5 per cent of the population at the moment is because it has perhaps made itself too aloof in the past, too remote and exclusive, and has not been prepared to meet all people at a human level.

I'm not sure that you gain anything by trying too hard to popularize it, or that you necessarily make the Gospels any more acceptable by gingering them up with guitar accompaniments. "Worship the Lord in the Beauty of Holiness" always seemed to me an appropriate approach to something which, after all, ought to be different from the mundane things of a material life. There ought to be a different standard, something to strive for.

So when I hear the bells of a distant church ringing out again on Sunday evening I can't help feeling torn, a feeling of is it for me or isn't it? Ought I to go, or shall I profit just as much by staying at home and enjoying the quietness here?

Those bells call with the eloquence of a John the Baptist. They have called Sunday after Sunday for a long time, challenging more doubts than mine; winning more arguments. Perhaps I ought to let them win again?

But I look out from my window and the garden is very still. I look at the sky and it is as calm as any chancel. I can't spoil this moment of peaceful expectancy by risking the journey to a church and then the disappointment I might find when I arrive. I tell myself that the bells are only this persuasive from a distance. If I stood beneath them now they would simply jar my senses with their discordant jangle. So don't go, says the silent room and the distance between my door and the church porch.

And so I have the same conflict tonight as I've had many times before. Because I cannot accept, I feel deprived. Because I cannot give in, I go without. Because I cannot accept what is there, ready-made, I wait and search for something I have not yet found.

I keep looking out of the window, staring at the sky, waiting. I notice how colourless the garden is. The flowers have finished. The leaves have fallen. There is a starkness and barrenness about it that seems right. Starlings have replaced the martins. The lawn is pocked with worm-casts. A cold wind sharpens the thorns.

Now the bells have stopped. It's too late to go now. In thousands of churches the belfries are roped into silence, the bells are made dumb and the service gets under way. Somewhere, the singing and the sharing are beginning again. Somewhere there is a place. . . .

My room is hauntingly still. I can hear my wrist-watch ticking. Outside, the world is almost frozen in its stillness. I feel inwardly excited by this sensation of stillness and solitary peace. And yet, at this moment, I still feel an emptiness. Somewhere there is an answer, in the dying sun or the tree's shadow.

> Out of this solitary service,
> staring hopefully into the white light
> of the sky where this day ends,
> I make some prayer. The sun
> drapes its embroidered cope
> before my eyes, the chancel
> of air down which I stare
> has something of mystery.
>
> But what of this garden now in shade,
> far from the sky's altar?
> The flowers cringe in the wind,
> the bird's praise is caught
> on the thorns of a rose-bush.
> All the symbols are here,
> but the heart still receives
> only the bread of despair.
>
> When darkness kneels where the sun
> knelt only an hour before,
> will the hand of sleep bestow
> what the day could not restore?
> And will the song that was caught
> on the cold thorns of fear
> blossom into the praise
> I sought for but could not hear?

The garden has become almost dark. Beyond the fence are the dark fields, the low endless fields of darkness lit only here and there by a lighted house, or a church where the service is coming to an end. I think again of the little church on Ten Mile Bank, or the one at Walpole St Peter.

I sit on, wondering why I force myself to accept this solitude and why, at the same time, I long to tear myself away from it to rush into the noise of a city. I begin to understand the paradox. As much as I need the silence of my room I need the confusion and brash lights of a city. I need to be one of a thousand faces going aimlessly between one distraction and another. I need to enjoy the anonymity of being just a face.

Until recently I always worked in a city for my living and I grew used to the rush and competitiveness of a society chasing more impressive results and even more bewildering statistics. And there were times when I enjoyed it all.

There are still times when I like being in cities, when I enjoy the bustle of streets and the excitement of going to a theatre or a concert. Train journeys can also give me almost as much pleasure as a country walk and being caught up in a crowd of strangers is not unlike looking over a new, strange landscape.

But having said that I still have to admit that I prefer these quiet hours alone with no craving for anything more than a few simple comforts and a long evening to let the mind wander while the body remains still. I can't go all the way with Thoreau who said, "I never found the companion that was so companionable as solitude," though I do agree with him when he says, "I know of but one or two persons with whom I can afford to walk. With most the walk degenerates into a more vigorous use of the legs."

To be alone and to want solitude is not to run away from life or to be selfish, ignoring any responsibility. It is a way of withdrawing a little from the scene in order to assess, to get things into perspective, to re-charge, so that one can continue to give back. Most creative people I suppose feel this necessity.

I draw back again and again into this landscape from which I have been taking for over twenty years. I need to walk out on familiar roads, to stand by a favourite stretch of water, or lean on a reliable gate. As I've said before it doesn't have to be very beautiful. It may not appeal to many people. But it's where I find the satisfaction and the strength to be what I want to be.

An old man with whom I sometimes share a gate and a long talk said to me the other day: 'We have to know our *own* value, what *our* life is worth. It's no use chasing after other people's notions. Success, in material terms, is no more than a good season.'

For me the values he was talking about are found in this landscape that I know is a part of me and of which I, in return, am also a part. What I find in the fields and skies of the fens cannot be devalued. It is an invisible bond between me and everyone else, between "time past and time future". When I handle the soil my blood quickens. When I breathe in the night air I am half intoxicated. When I look up at the stars we are not separated by millions of miles or years but are all one, all part of the great rhythm and life of the universe. We may not be here for long. Our life may not be more than a second in that universe, but it is an important second and equally important that we should know of our contribution.

Week-days

Two days have passed and there is a new moon, the last of this season. My occasional visits to Impington Village College have started again and suddenly my involvement with other people, both in schools and at adult education classes, make me question the confused thoughts of a few days ago.

Driving through the fens once more I feel the excitement of being on familiar roads again and of going back into a classroom to work with children. Perhaps this excitement is generated by the energy and ideas I have stored up during the idle summer and solitary walks, but now I find myself keyed-up and anxious to be with people again.

The day is bright with a clarity of light that gives sharp outlines to buildings and intensifies the colour of bricks, tiles, barns and gates. The sky is more of a pale mauve than blue. The air has a cleanness that you can taste. The threat of an autumn fog did not materialize. There was a heavy dew at daybreak but soon the air was as sharp as crystal. The lapwings are back and this morning I counted seventy-three along the river-bank. I see a troupe of them now somersaulting in a field where a man is plough-ing, the white flashes of their wings reflecting the sunlight as they tumble and twist through their acrobatics. What a good day it is to be out. Ely cathedral shines on the horizon as I continue my drive eastward and turn towards Haddenham, Wilburton and on to Twentypence Road. I stop my car at the usual gateway near the inn and walk down to the river. A few boats are still moored there, their reflections perfectly reproduced in the calm water. There is a lovely early October smell to the morning, a morning that is a positive and triumphant proclamation of life. The grass is wet and my face feels the delicate touch of wonder as I walk through invisible spiders' webs strung from one hedge to another across my path. These few moments are enough to get the mind toned-up for the day's work and I am anxious to be on my way to share the day with youngsters who are quicker to respond to the world's excitement than I was at their age.

At the end of the afternoon Neville and Muriel Williams, who teach at the Village College, invite me home for tea. Their love of books, music and the countryside does not make tea an ordinary meal. Although the move from the table after more than an hour indicates that tea is over our talk goes on between cups of tea for another six hours and it is half-past ten before I leave for home. We have been to Yorkshire, the Lake District, Wales and Dorset. We have talked about Wordsworth, Dylan Thomas and Thomas Hardy, and have swapped anecdotes that have reawakened memories unpremeditated at half-past four.

When I get out into the darkness and drive off I suddenly realize that it's been a long day and that I'm very tired, the kind of tiredness that is a pleasure when it comes after such well-spent hours.

The year itself seems to have grown older since the morning. A low mist hovers over the fields and creates phantoms in the hedgerows. The hedges themselves look more autumnal now in the night than they did at the day's beginning. As the car headlights scythe along the grass verges and bushes they have a yellowness that presages the season's great leaf-fall. The hawthorns especially look well-advanced into old age and the chestnuts are already showing the anatomy of their branches.

This is one of the sensations I enjoy most from driving—going home late at night between hedgerows or an avenue of trees and seeing the eerie patterns created by the car's lights. It makes a world of fantasy. The trunks of the trees are a different colour. The branches are a different shape. There are unexpected shadows and brief glimmerings in spinneys. The hour is full of ghosts. The night pleasantly haunted. Patches of mist cling near corners or slip through farm-gates, friendly spectres add a chilling magic to the ride. And it is a landscape that knows many ghosts. The fen country has a long tradition of telling ghost stories. They're easy to believe on such a night.

In a few weeks' time these mists may well be thick fogs and the trees will be bare. There will be no joy then in such a night journey. But now these vapours play at hide-and-seek and the air is clear enough to reveal bright stars. I stop for a moment and look up at the familiar constellations returning to their usual positions in the heavens. There they were, the "fire-folk" of Gerard Manley Hopkins, "The bright boroughs, the circle-citadels . . ." reassuring, ever-lasting, faithful, dependable. The same stars seen by Cornelius Vermuyden more than three hundred years ago. The same stars seen by Hereward the Wake and William the Conqueror nine hundred years away, before the fens were drained or roads existed between these villages. A ghostly barn-owl swooped by, out of the mist and into the mist. A pheasant's cry made me shiver. It was nearly midnight.

Wind

The autumn so far is very uncertain and its days are unpredictable. Conditions change overnight. Even hours are different seasons. One day is calm and filled with sunlight. The next day can be dull and wintry with strong winds.

Today has been a day when the winds have reached gale force. Trees have been ripped out of the ground. Fences have been blown down. Gates swing open on broken hinges and the streets are littered with roof-tiles and garden debris. Apples that were ready for picking and waiting for labourers have now been shaken out of the trees. The orchards are full of bruises.

Low black clouds are still being buffeted about the sky like boats in harbour. They bump and groan, spilling great splashes of rain that whip the ground and scratch the window panes.

Drivers have been warned not to drive too fast or travel on exposed roads. How would I get to Spalding today, I wonder, or Ramsey or Chatteris. I know that in this weather I would be afraid to drive along Deeping High Bank or Ramsey Forty Foot. On that particular tightrope of a road you would be lucky to keep your balance in a ten-ton tank. A car would be blown off the road and into the drain or fields in seconds—a considerable drop whichever way you went.

We can combat snow and rain. We can control floods. We can put out fires. But we sit helplessly listening to the wind straining at the windows to get in, thundering down the chimney, slamming doors and making walls tremble. Nothing in this landscape makes a man feel so defeated. In the spring a farmer must stand by utterly helpless and watch his seeds torn out of the ground and blown away in one of the dust storms I've spoken of before. In winter he can keep a close eye on the fresh water coming into the fens from the uplands and wait anxiously for each high tide. He can control the flow of water through the sluices and into the rivers. But when the wind blows as it blows today these fears are multiplied. You cannot build sea-walls or sluice-gates against the wind. It attacks across the whole breadth of the land. It is the invisible enemy.

Tomorrow, if it's fine, we shall be out gleaning some comfort from today's damage, looking for fallen branches that will fit into the boot of the car and which we can saw up for winter logs. Boys will be out too in the parks and along roadsides looking for conkers. I shall look for them too, for there is nothing more enjoyable in October than collecting conkers. Their thick green shells cracked open on the paths or verges, the bright shining fruit inside as wonderful as a new-born foal. There is a newness about the year's first conkers that takes some beating. The colour of the nut has such a richness, such a jewel-like finish. It is the next best thing to seeing a chicken hatch from its shell in the spring. The revelation and perfection of birth.

Night comes early. We light lamps, draw curtains and try to shut out the day's wildness by listening to music. Not the windswept music of Sibelius or the stormy music of Beethoven, but the pure, unearthly sounds of Purcell.

Moons and Exiles

As if to tease the mind this erratic month suddenly produces an evening of such calm that the trees look as if they have not moved a leaf since summer. Their colour has changed but most of them have clung to the branches during the last few days of wind and now they hang limp and still. There is a full moon in a clear sky and a theatrical lighting over the park with its lawns, gardens and great variety of trees.

I have spent the evening with the Scottish author, Hugh Douglas, and we talked through until the early hours of the morning. It's nearly always about writing and the ways in which we draw our material from different sources.

'There are times,' Hugh said, 'when I envy you having your own native landscape right on your doorstep. I can see now that it makes a lot of difference.'

'You mean you're feeling homesick at last?'

'No, it's not so much homesickness, though I suppose we all feel that. I've lived away from Scotland now for nearly twenty years but I always want to write about it in the way that you are writing about the fens.'

'But you're doing that, surely? After all, you've written five books about Scotland, including two of your favourite subjects—Robert Burns and Bonnie Prince Charlie.'

'Yes, I agree, but I still feel they're books coming from the "outside", from a distance, if you like. You must remember that I am a bit of an exile now and it's easy to lose touch, easy to lose the feel of a place. That's why I envy you. When you want more than facts you can go out and sit on the edge of a field and watch the land and the people working. You can meet them, talk to them, see them every day of the year and understand them. They're always there, and so are you. That's what I mean when I say I really ought to go back.'

We refill the whisky glasses and continue to discuss the importance of a landscape, the importance of knowing where you want to draw your material from all the time, how writing about a particular landscape means going beyond words, beyond language. I remembered what Charles Kingsley had written in his essay *My Winter Garden*—"It is pleasant and good to see the same trees year after year, the same birds coming back in spring to the same shrubs, the same banks covered with the same flowers . . ." and I realized that the "good thing" about this familiarity was that it enabled one to take that much for granted and go beyond it, or deeper into it, where there were new discoveries to be made beneath the surface.

'If I could go back for just a few months,' continued Hugh, 'I feel I could get a book from the "inside" for a change, from the real me on my own soil. You've never had this feeling of exile, have you, have never been away from your native surroundings long enough to know just how much you can miss them? I feel it now so deeply that it hurts. Here I am, a Scot living in Peterborough, working in London, writing about Ayrshire. . . . It's like living in a Time Machine.'

'You'd better start writing about the fens,' I said cautiously.

'And you must be joking. At least we're good friends now—we might not be then.'

We were finally left with only ice-cubes and an empty bottle and so we let our ambitions trail off into hazy longings and vague intentions about the next book after the next book and how long could we go on pounding the typewriter in the hope of increasing our royalties enough to keep up with "threshold agreements".

When Hugh saw me to the door I was only five minutes from home. The night was big and still. The sky was golden-blue. The stars pale. I walked round the outside of the park. The trees shadowed me. There was no sound, not even an owl. I couldn't help looking at the moon. The knowledge that Man has been up there now with his marvellous machines has not made it any less beautiful or romantic. On a night like this when it is full and proud it still beckons the mind to make its own journeys, journeys far more exciting than any ever made by rockets. The moon offers such silence. With the speed of light my mind went to a dozen places where I had been similarly spellbound by its presence—to a night in Switzerland when I saw it glazing the snow on the mountains across Lake Brienz; to a time when I was crossing from the Isle of Wight on the night-ferry and the sea was golden; to a night in Cumberland when about a dozen of us, all strangers, stood on Friar's Crag and watched it dip into Borrowdale; or a winter's evening at Stonehenge when all the land was covered with a white frost that glistened in that flood-lit, moon-lit silence.

Old people still have their superstitions about the moon. It not only governs the tides of the sea but the affairs of men, and of individual behaviour. I was talking to a lady recently who can remember her mother curtseying to a new moon. As children we used to spit at it for luck and older people would turn their money over. There were proverbs too about the moon that I heard quoted often as a child:

> Always kill your pig when the moon is waxing
> Never wait to kill till the moon is full.

or

> Sow peas and beans in the wane of the moon,
> Who soweth them sooner soweth too soon.

Fifty years ago my father and grandfather kept pigs and never had a pig killed during full moon; my grandfather put great store by the phases of the moon and would only sow his seeds at certain times.

The man in the moon was a real person too. For some he was a wicked old man condemned to carry a bundle on his back for ever more. For the children in our street he was the sleepy old gnome and keeper of dreams. You could never dream when there was no moon, for the old gnome was then visiting another country.

No, we have not much
for the impatient eye or ear.
When the sky grows colourless
there is only this deep mirror
you call space into which we peer
when the day is over . . .

Standing there, staring up at the moon that has now been visited and made gnomeless, I couldn't help thinking of that man in the fens whom I knew well and who would not believe that mortal man had travelled through space to land on that small golden orb that had been there since Genesis.

> For seventy years he's watched the new crops grow
> but has not felt his roots get pot-bound in
> the fen's black soil. His eyes, trained on a far
> horizon, are still bird-bright, and yet his mind's
> as narrow as Vermuyden's drain. He has not shared
> those pleasures we have made for our amusement;
> has never been to a theatre, cinema, or read a book.
> When aircraft chalk graffiti on his sky he says
> 'I think they're tempting Providence.' (I'm not sure
> whether he means for flying or for writing on God's wall.)
> When men walked for the first time on the moon
> he'd not believe such crazy rumours could deceive
> people he'd always thought intelligent. Coaxed at last
> into a neighbour's house to watch the second-landing
> on TV all he could say, when faced with such
> convincing evidence as bouncing astronauts, was
> 'have you seen men with legs as short as that? Not me.'
>
> Walking back home he looked across the fields,
> his roots more deeply-planted now in what he knows,
> his world revolving slowly round a farm where
> every day his mortal years are tempting Providence.

Beyond the outskirts of the town now those low black fields would be just as silent and full of secrets. The water in the dykes would be bright from the same moon, the night filled with the same magic. I could see that land. I knew each farm and house. I knew the people. It was all familiar. It would all be there in the morning.

I had to admit, Scotland felt a very long, long way away. It must have felt even longer for someone like Hugh Douglas.

Into White Silence

When autumn ages into winter no other season can offer such stillness. There are other degrees of stillness in other seasons, but none can equal the complete motionless, breathless, silent stillness of an autumn morning in mist. There is no hint of the expectancy that you feel in spring and no threat yet of the snow that might come in winter; and the stillness that broods over the land before a heat storm in summer is quite different. No, this tense, grey stillness comes from the mist itself and the loss of space. Familiar landmarks disappear or become so blurred in the near distance that they lose their identity and sense of belonging.

Walking over the Washlands towards the River Nene this morning I stop to breathe in the pungent smell of damp vegetation. There is a sweetness to the rankness, and something ordered and perfect in its wildness. This is a real fenland smell. It is powerful and primeval. You'd never think that the fens had been drained for more than three hundred years. The dampness eats into you. The mist wraps round you. The smell seeps into your clothes like bonfire smoke. It is a day on which civilization has hardly left its mark.

I stand still for several moments and am absorbed by the mist, by the smell and the damp. The bones ache with the memory of what it used to be like in the fens before they were drained, when men took opium to ease their ague, when for nearly half the winter they had to walk about on stilts to get from field to field, or from street to street, or even to walk about in their own one-storey houses that would be flooded several times during the winter months.

It's strange to feel this link with them as I walk through the low clinging mist. The legs feel heavier and have to push. The feet go down tentatively. It's almost like walking through invisible snow. Already the town lies hidden behind me. The tall spire of St Mary's church, usually seen from ten miles away, cannot be seen from a mile's distance. The island of willow trees rests like a grey, earth-bound cloud on the land, a cloud that no wind will ever blow away.

Willow trees are essential to this landscape. Their foliage and shape, their bark and sturdiness are typical features of the fens' character. They add no brazen colour to the season's usual display of gaudy leaves and hold less prominence in other countrysides. But here, near the water, as part of the water, they have a stark, uncompromising beauty that I like, and if Whittlesey had not been called Witelsig after a Saxon landowner by the name of Witel then I'm sure that Willow Isle would have been an adequate alternative many years ago.

I continue my walk towards the river. Cattle stand outlined on the bank. They too look as ancient as Saxon England. The river is very high today, several feet above normal, and the cattle are forced on to the higher ground of the bank. The fields too are showing large areas of flooding. Swans have taken over from the cattle and now feed on the swampy marshland.

The river is perfectly still, holding the reflection of the pylons without blurring their outline. The surface of the water is not even disturbed by the rising air-bubbles from fish or eel on the river-bed. No insects settle on the liquid glass. No birds fly over. There is just this total, complete, timeless stillness of an early grey morning in an ageing autumn.

I wait for a long time by the water, waiting for some strange and ancient god to emerge from the mist of his long sleep. What if some tribal lord of six thousand years ago had been buried and preserved like a bog-oak? What if he suddenly appeared and in the cold morning air began to breathe? What would I learn? Or how quickly would I run back to the hopeful safety of my house?

The stillness is at last broken by the arrival of a heron, a grey lordly heron who settles fifty feet away at the water's edge and in that moment dramatically demolishes the pylon's reflection which, in the stillness, I'd forgotten wasn't real.

It is going to be a grey-mist day all day. Already the mist thickens and the air gets cooler. The fields look wetter and blacker, more cruel and untameable. They are going back to their origins. They are going to win. It is a day on which there will be no light, no great skies, no bright space or far horizons. This is going to be a different fenland, one perhaps to which you have to be born, or out of which you have to come. It is a day on which you need the mist to hide the sullen fields and uncomfortable work.

> You need it sometimes,
> not for the pretty picture that it makes
> for the romantic eye,
> but to hide the harshness of those weeks
> when barren fields will draw
> the last warm blood-cell from your limbs

and you can feel the teeth
of wet earth feeding on your legs and arms.

You need it when the roads
are thick with mud and grass is black
from winter's heavy wheels,
when dark rain fills each narrow dyke
and summer's crops are part
of memory. You need the mist
on such a day when cold
cracks through your skin and eyes cry frost.

I know there have been times
when I have praised a different view
making a world out of
its fantasy, making it glow.
Not now. The pain aches more
each bleak November day comes back.
These flooded fields are facts
and I have seen the spirits they can break.

Last night frost came into the mist and this morning all the rooftops are white. The fences, gates, lawns and garden sheds are all covered in silvery rime that transforms them completely. It is cold still and the sky rests on the chimney-pots.

I have made no plans for going out today and the house is going to be empty for the whole of the day. I know I shall get claustrophobia listening for sounds that are not there, waiting for people who won't come, growing irritable in my own company.

The house feels as if its been empty for years, and it's only hours. On a cold, grey, long and silent morning like this the unshared hours multiply and the few words I scribble down spasmodically will not keep on a straight line.

Hours spent alone in the country or by the riverside are never this lonely, never lonely in the same way that a house is lonely. The silence under the stars at midnight or the sun at noon-day is never as tense as it is under a white ceiling.

I sit listening to the silence. Each click jabs at my senses. Each tick of my watch grows in volume. I can neither work nor read. I am too aware of being here in this room on my own. Eventually out of this unrest comes a poem.

Next door my neighbours are listening
to their radio. Music so faint I strain
my hearing to enjoy the distance now
that separates their world from mine.

And something in the fragments that I hear
brings back a moment when this room was shared,
when we had music played so quietly
that only we knew what was heard.

But now this room is silent and outside
dry leaves are shuffling round the gate
like prying children trying to get in.
The house by memory's made so desolate.

The moment is as sharp as any thorn
exposed by winter. In such frail moods
I dare not move for fear the thought is torn.
I dare not speak in case the silence bleeds.

I lose track of time until I notice that the fire is nearly out. I clear the
ashes and put on some small logs. Then I stand at the window and watch
the dry leaves nudge each other and scuttle away when they see me. The
poem made me see them that way and gave some meaning to the morning's inactivity.

The sky is still desolate and continues so into the afternoon. I feel myself
mesmerized by the stillness and have no power to break out into the
street, no power to find sound that will end this stillness.

Rain

So many elements and sensations in so brief a time. The days do not
belong to the same week or month but grow out of their own making.

I spent some time this morning talking to a man when I should have
been in a hurry. In fact I *was* in a hurry and very anxious to get away. But
I also wanted to spend half-an-hour with this man if I could, for he is a
good talker.

He could see my uneasiness. 'A-yew dying to go somewhere?'

I wasn't quite sure how to answer this ambiguous question but said,
'Well, I mustn't be too long, I've got a lot to do today.'

'Then yew wanna slow yerself down a bit. That's 'arf the trouble with people today, they're in more hurry than there's time.'

'And I bet that's just what people used to say to you when you were younger, isn't it?'

'No, I don't think so . . . yew couldn't go much faster than your old 'oss and cart would let you go. Life's a lot quicker now what wi' yer motor cars and all this tearing about, it's no wonder young fellers 'ave 'eart-attacks and die afore they're any age at all.'

Somehow we got on to inflation. I think it started with him grumbling about the price of a new Harris tweed jacket he'd just bought—the first for several years. The shock had nearly given him a heart attack. Then we switched from jackets to funerals.

'It's the same wi' burials,' he said. 'When we buried my poor ol' mother we 'ad a hearse and two cars, plus all the undertaker's fees and the lot didn't come to ten quid. Today yer wouldn't get that for a hundered and ten . . . and let's face it, they don't make coffins to last these days, do they!'

The navy-blue clouds piled up on the horizon and there were the first few drops of rain exploding like tiny wine-glasses on the dry pavement.

'It doesn't look too promising,' I said.

'No, that's gooin' to be a wet day all day if that rain's coming this way . . . yew ain't gooin' to do a lot o' gallivanting today if yew arsk me.'

He had a real fenland accent with rising cadences at the end of each phrase or sentence and a good mixture of dialect words to spice his talk. I could have stayed listening for another hour but I made my escape at a suitable opportunity.

Quite a lot of dialect words are still commonly used by some of the older people I meet and my own father uses them frequently when we're having a conversation. Words like *pingle*, which means to eat without appetite or enthusiasm, to just pick at your food instead of getting on with it; or *clart*, which means to get messed-up or to make something sticky. The word *frez* is often used for frozen and the word *pitcher* is still used for a jug. Gypsies are known as *didecoys*; to *chunter* is to moan and *enow* means enough. The word *frit* means frightened and *fardin'* is still used when old people talk about farthings, or *fippence* when they talk about fivepence. To get something the wrong-way round is to get it *cross-wobbled*, and *blar-me* is an expression used as often as *good lork-a-day*.

The rain became more than a threat and settled in for the day. I was beginning to see I may not be doing as much "gallivanting" as I'd planned, but the thought of rain on my face made me suddenly long to be out in the fens, walking in the pouring rain, to feel again the sweet coolness of the water from the skies. My mind went back to a day when I had been away from this landscape for a long time and the first thing I wanted to do was to go for a long walk on the roads and paths I'd known as a child. . . .

I walked past the church and the little bridge, past the pubs and the railway lines, out once more into the wild fens. No one else was about. The world looked more desolate than I had remembered and the weight of rain on the trees made them heavy and motionless. When I'd walked about half a mile down the road I stood and held my head back so that the rain could fall full on my face. I stayed like that for several seconds with my eyes closed, looking up at the sky I could not see, letting the rain fall steadily over me until the water ran in little streams off my cheeks, down my neck and under my collar. My hair was soaked and I could feel the water seeping through my clothes. When I opened my mouth the rain trickled in and I tasted the earth and the clouds, the sun and the sky, the winds and the grass that had gone into that sip of a thousand years. Slowly I forgot the smells of a city's factories and traffic and smelt instead that lovely fresh smell of the land under rain. I heard the soft hissing sound of the leaves drinking in the water and the earth breathing in the wet. It smelt the purest wet ever known since ice and fire met. When I opened my eyes the low clouds and the empty fields spoke of such freedom that I began running and singing, skipping and shouting like a child on a seashore. Slugs and snails peered out from the drenched spears of grass. Rooks laughed from nearby elm trees. A moorhen took fright and panicked away down the narrow dyke. In the distance the brickyard chimneys were lost in the low clouds. But I was so happy to be back on that patch of earth that I ran and skipped all the way back to the railway-crossing and into my home street. When I reached the house I was completely wet through, my shoes were like sponges, my jacket like a potato sack. But at least I felt clean again.

All that was a long time ago, but the memory of my joy that day came back to me as I thought of walking out in the rain again some thirty years later. There was not the same naïve ecstasy but I stayed out long enough to feel the sweetness and the silence of rain, to feel the immediate dampness of this land as soon as rain falls. The earth looked blacker than ever, the horizon more of a mirage than a reality. Already the washlands were holding huge pools of water, growing slowly into winter floods ready, perhaps, for skating. The only part of the day that shone was the grass on the river banks. It was luminous. It had a wet-green, rain-green newness about it as though no dust had ever settled on its blades. It made me

thankful again for the "wildness and wet" of this landscape. I stood looking at it for several minutes, breathing the damp air, feeling again the
wetness getting through to my skin, feeling the rain soak through my hair
and run down my neck. The grass became more living than I had ever
seen it before. I thought I could see it growing, moving like some huge
beast towards a new rebirth or evolution. The grass breathed. The grass
had heart-beats. The grass watched. It had eyes.

Around me was a world of misty greyness, layers of skin being shed by
this new creation. I was almost afraid to move, to step back, to walk away.
Even now, sitting beside my fire and recollecting the day, I can't forget
it. It stays in my mind, bright-green and shining. It will be praised again
and again in spring when it reawakens from its parched winter and when
it becomes golden with buttercups in early summer. But it will never be
more vivid, more potent, more full of mystery and ancient seasons than it
was today.

St Luke's Little Summer

We do not live in a part of England where autumn can make an ostentatious display of its leaving. We cannot look out over tree-filled valleys
and marvel at the fantasies exhibited by millions of leaves adding their
own shades of yellow, orange, red, brown and golden to the remaining
greens. Our autumns do not come on such big canvases. They cannot
equal those I have seen in Worcestershire and Cumbria, in Gloucestershire
and Wales. In those places the leaf-fall is among nature's most spectacular
gifts. We have to be satisfied with such autumns in miniature—a cluster
of trees that blaze like fires in their isolation against the vivid blue sky, a
hedgerow of fruit that could easily be overlooked in a more generous part
of the country.

Autumn is more than falling leaves. It is a season of fulfilment, a season
of unwinding, or slowing down for the winter, a feeling of contentment
if the year has been good and a time to be philosophical if it hasn't. It is a
time when the mornings awake slowly out of their mists and the skies
clear to become crystal bright. The fields change. The land looks and
smells different. The days are shorter and end in blue smoke rising from
old chimneys as the first fires are lit.

Time and time again we notice how, by about the middle of October,
we are blessed with a brief spell of warm days that, like an encore to a

summer already forgotten, hold up the progress of the year, preventing the winter from entering too soon.

Today was Sunday and the morning insisted that all the jobs to be done, all the plans that were made for other tasks, should be abandoned and that we should go out into the countryside to make sure of this celebration.

We travelled towards the western boundary of the fens and it was not long before we were on quiet narrow roads picking the last blackberries of the year. The October sun was warm on our backs and as we picked the soft fruit from the briars the berries were also warm to the touch, warm and ripe enough to stain the fingers with their juice, adding a sweet smell to the morning air.

All round us in distant villages we could hear church-bells ringing—in Castor, Ufford, Wansford, Barnack—their far-off silvery sounds coming over the fields, sometimes fading away, sometimes being blown nearer on a wave of wind. It was not "summertime on Bredon" but like the bells in Housman's poem they were "a happy noise to hear". They even prompted a skylark to rise into the shining, echoing air to peal his own carillon in competition with those of St Kyneburga of Castor.

The hedgerows from which we were picking had either not been discovered or were extremely prolific with the season's fruit. The blackberries hung down in heavy clusters. The hips were fat and bright as poppies. The haws so thick on some bushes that they glowed like furnaces. Here and there Old Man's Beard or a sprig of Traveller's Joy gave variety to a roadside that had clumps of nettles, banks of ivy, bushes, weeds and flowers that suggested that the hedges had been there for over five hundred years. A world in miniature, but enough to remind us again of one of the year's greatest pleasures even though our autumns cannot compete with those where woods are taken for granted.

Nothing satisfies the soul quite so much as blackberrying on a quiet sun-lit morning in October. Your shoes may get soaked from the grass and your old jacket may get skegged on the thorns, the hands will be stung by the nettles and the back will ache from trying to reach too high for the unattainable fruit. But oh, the feeling of refreshment, of ease, of relaxation, of satisfaction! We filled two containers—enough to go with the fallen apples we'd been given so that we could have a home-made apple pie big enough to see us through the week.

The road led over old common land and through farmyards until we came once more to a village with its white-washed pub, not yet open, and the church bells now silent. Nearby was a small pond and some ducks. Sheep grazed at the edge of fields that bordered the street. It could have been a morning from the eighteenth century. It could have been a Samuel Palmer picture come to life.

White cumulus drifted in from the northern sky, dazzling snow-drifts of clouds that bruised the eyes with their glare. The air grew cooler with them. They reminded us of the frailty of the season, a season that knows it must live each day at this burning intensity, for it can only live in the failing present, can only look back on its past. The spring knows what is to come. The summer need not hurry. But autumn must contribute its measure in days already threatened by winter.

The man who must look after his land and prepare his fields for other seasons also knows what is to be done. No sooner are the harvest crops in than work must begin again preparing for next year. To the farm-worker the seasons must still mean more than they do to most men. Every job has its own time, its right time. Ploughing in the autumn, when the land needs turning over for the winter, suddenly changes the colour and pattern of this landscape. Fields that only a few weeks ago were yellow and golden with straw now become black with long straight furrows of rich soil that glistens like slabs of melting tar in the sun.

Men still take pride in ploughing, too. The tractor may have replaced the horse but a straight furrow and an even field continue to give a man satisfaction. I knew a farm foreman who once sacked a man because he couldn't plough straight. 'It's all right for him,' he said, 'he can go home at nights, but I've got to live with it. I'd be ashamed to let anyone know it was mine.' And when he said "straight" he wanted the furrows of his fields to look as if they'd been measured and drawn by a ruler.

> Look at that rich earth.
> There are no stones defacing
> those furrows or fine crops.
> Straight as jet-black corduroy
> it has been cared-for more than
> the Sunday-suit of the proud man
> who stands with penetrating eyes
> judging each row. His face
> might have been that of Michelangelo
> who could not hide his pride
> under the shutters of tired flesh.
>
> Born seventy years ago
> this man has worked at his trade

coaxing art out of his black soil
until he knows each clod, each
chisel-mark of the sharp plough.
That is enough. He wants no more
than what his fields can give,
no more than their perfection
and the bare comforts of his home
smelling each night of bacon and the smoke
that's always rising from a well-made fire.

This year's brief autumn could not have reached its perfection on a better day, as I returned to Impington Village College and a reunion school-dinner with the youngsters with whom I had worked earlier in the year.

The day began with a low mist and a hazy sun, but by the time I had reached Sutton-in-the-Isle the sky was brightening and the colours in the trees were extravagantly vivid. Soon the air cleared completely and the October day showed again how theatrical it could be, not only in its great stage presence but also in its ambitious production. Here at last was the full pageantry of the tragic season, dying in drapes of gold, making its final speech against a fanfare of branches.

The day's excitement had an unexpected bonus as I drove into Cottenham and saw the amusements and sideshows of Cottenham Feast on the village green. The brightly coloured tents and caravans, the swinging-boats and roundabouts, all encircled by the yellowing trees, presented a scene as timeless as one could ever wish to see. This was a part of the continuing history and tradition of English village life that has been going on for a thousand years.

When I reached Histon there was no Fair on the village green but the colours in the row of chestnut trees along the road to Girton forced me to make a diversion. The richness of the dying foliage was so dazzling that it appeared unreal. And yet no imagination could have conceived such a decor or made such a grand gesture. Not even the funerals of a dozen pharaohs and a score of kings could have lavished so much gold and such splendour on their roads to immortality. St Luke's Little Summer had succeeded again.

Later

Now, a week later, there is little of autumn left. Several days of strong winds have stripped the trees nearly bare. The hedgerows have prepared their thorns for winter. The lapwings are back on the land. I went for a walk this morning and watched the final destruction of leaves in the park. The paths were thick with them. They flurried around frantically like birds unable to fly. When a forceful gust of wind shook a nearby tree a whole aviary of leaves blew out of the branches leaving the tree's cage empty. They settled on the grass for a moment and then scurried off to join the others on the path.

PART THREE

THE ESSENTIAL WINTER

"I wish to hear the silence of the night,
for silence is something positive to be heard."
Thoreau: Jan 21st 1853

Journeys

THERE IS A different silence on the land now. The translucent light has gone and there is only the endless, depressing, damp and unbreakable sky brooding over us like a prison guard with folded arms and tight lips.

The rain is almost incidental. The land is wet, the sky is wet and the rain is only wind-blown water that flows between these grey worlds of wet. The grass verges are coated with mud from the lorries taking the sugar-beet to the British Sugar Corporation factories. Sugar-beet is surely the least attractive crop of all, from sowing to lifting. In the spring it may need several drillings before the dry winds give it chance to germinate. Its care offers the farm-worker one of the most monotonous jobs in the land. It is also a crop very prone to a disease causing a low tonnage crop with a reduced sugar content. It is not particularly attractive to look at when growing and it is harvested in the bleakest months of the year when the land is either too soft from rain, or too hard from frost.

If it's a wet season the fen roads get slimy with the mud brought out of the fields by the lorries and trailers and the smell from the sugar-beet factories hangs like a doom-laden cloud over the town for weeks. Newcomers sniff the air and look quizzically at passers-by. To discover this landscape for the first time in November can put you off for life—unless, of course, it happens to be a November of fields and hedges made white by frost.

To walk out on such a morning when the grass crunches like broken glass beneath your feet, when the air is keen and appetizing, when the water in the dykes reflects the blueness of the sky and the fields are coated with rime then it is as beautiful as at any other time of the year. Certainly it is a necessary part of the year. The land wilts that does not know frost between summer and spring.

One of the miracles at this time is when frost and mist come together; for then every stalk, every twig, every reed and blade of green becomes silver-plated and glistens in the hazy light. To be first out on those winter roads, when either your footprints or tyre-tracks are the only marks left behind you on the white-powdered surface, is to feel an excitement, a sensation that cannot be equalled in any other season. To see the frozen mist on everything from a cobweb to a farm-gate over such a vast landscape is to be transported to a world so wholly white that it could be a different continent. The trees bow, heavy with their brief adornment. The furrows have teeth of polished steel. Even the sheep standing forlornly along the river-bank have been changed, or dressed in costume. The mist has clung to their long wool and the frost has knitted them a coat of glass. When they run a few paces the dangling icicles tinkle like Chinese bells.

I remember that morning when I stopped on the North Bank to talk to an old man who had been a shepherd and had seen such a morning many times, taking the enhanced world very much for granted. He expected each season to be different and all the transformations brought about by a frosty morning were quite natural. For him, I once wrote:

> . . . a lark singing through mist
> was simply a lark, even though ice
> clouded the air and the grass was frozen.
>
> Sheep with rime caked on their backs
> were just sheep who had grazed out all night
> under frost that was perfectly natural.
>
> And when the guttural croak of a pheasant
> cracked over the water it was an echo
> your ears took for granted . . .

But today is not that sort of day. I dwell too much on hope and forget the bleakness and lack of beauty on this grey, wet morning when something more than affection holds both body and spirit loyal to the land.

Already the low pasture fields are flooded and return for a while to their primitive marshiness. Lapwings swoop and tumble through the rain, trying to outwit their reflections in the water below. Swans grow in number and today I count fifty-three.

My day has to be shared equally between the town of March and the city of Ely. March has a history of mixed fortunes both before and since its great days as one of the biggest marshalling yards for the railway in Europe. In the eleventh century it was a small hamlet of about fifty people. The old, and then only course of the River Nene flowed between its rows of cottages. By the thirteenth century it had grown into a small market town and began attracting trade, both by road and river. Barges tied up at its quay and travelling salesmen walked through the streets calling out their wares. But March never became a Wisbech or a King's Lynn, and its life for the next three hundred years was comparatively quiet. It's revival and growth came in the boom days of the railways where it was strategically placed in the fens for linking up many of the eastern region's passenger and freight lines. Not only was it in a good position for the railway companies but it was also able to offer an area of relatively poor land by fenland standards which meant that as well as the station there could also be extensive marshalling yards for goods traffic. March became, as Swindon and Crewe were to become, a new town for a new age—the age of steam transport. By the 1930s it was one of the major railway junctions in East Anglia and the largest marshalling yard in the country with miles of tracks and sidings.

The town grew and changed rapidly, as all towns do when some form of revolution like this takes place, whether it's in coal-mining areas, or engineering centres, or now those previously neglected corners of northeast Scotland where the oil-rigs are the symbols of a new revolution. New houses, new schools, new chapels and halls were built for the people arriving from all parts of England to live and work for the railway companies. March soon had its brass bands and choirs and the new population quickly fashioned itself into a virile and independent community, a community that no longer remained typically "fenland", though March folk still like to believe they are fenmen to the core. The River Nene had also been rerouted long before the railways came and the town was left with a docile, narrow tentacle of water that really had nowhere to go. When the railways were drastically reduced and many of the Eastern Region's services cancelled, March had to partly reorientate itself to a mixture of agriculture and light industry. But once again it is a busy, interesting and expanding town with enough character to last for a few more generations.

What has remained throughout all these periods of change is the church of St Wendreda, rightly renowned for the double hammerbeam angel roof—a canopy of spread wings that give the impression that the roof is actually moving, there are that many wings.

Fortunately railways still run through March and provide a choice of remarkable rides over the fens, whether you go from Peterborough to Ely and Cambridge or up to King's Lynn. Because the fens have dropped in level so much over the years and the railway lines have been maintained at their original levels you get those wonderful panoramic views from the carriage windows. There are no traffic worries either, no traffic queues in towns, no forbidding signs saying you can't turn right or left, no responsibilities at all. You can just sit back and enjoy the ride over rich fertile plains where each season can be seen in immense magnificence.

Many of the little stations have, perhaps accidentally, preserved some relics of the past—rows of red fire-buckets that have been hanging outside the Gents for a hundred years; platform seats whose iron legs are sturdily fashioned in the initials of the railway company—GNR or GER; station gas-lamps and Victorian waiting-rooms; iron foot-bridges and old post-boxes; things that have either defied, or been overlooked by, British Rail.

I still love travelling by rail and get a peculiar pleasure out of some of the remaining branch lines. I've never been a "steam engine addict" but I suppose it's all to do with nostalgia. I seldom travel from Peterborough to March without remembering my journeys as a boy from Whittlesey to Hunstanton when we went on holidays. The thrill of walking down to the little station at the very rim of the town comes back to me as if it happened only yesterday, instead of forty years ago. . . .

When we were within sight of the railways I would run on ahead to get to the station first. I would stand at the white gates and listen to the bells inside the gate-keeper's hut, then run along the path and on to the platform where the porter waited with a trolley and some luggage. I would look up at the still-burning, pale-yellow gas-lamps hanging from the roof. I would stare at the row of red fire-buckets. I would wait for my father to arrive at the ticket office, and then I would look impatiently at the two shining rails that curved away into a unifying distance out of which would come the train. The rails remained empty for a long while. The porter looked at his watch. The grown-ups paced slowly backwards and forwards. I looked at the signals and then studied the distance for a blur of smoke that would announce the arrival of the steam train along those gleaming rails.

We climbed noisily and excitedly into the corridorless compartments. We heard the whistle blow and felt the carriages shuffle into motion. Soon the town was left behind as the train gathered speed. To begin with I would examine the water-colours of castles or harbours that hung above the long seats. Our buckets and spades, towels and sandwiches were stacked on to the corded luggage rack that sagged with so many holiday trips I thought it would not last the journey. Having decided which of the pictures I liked best I would then move from one side of the carriage to the other to look out of the windows. I was always facinated to watch the rise and fall of the telegraph wires between their poles. It gave me the sensation of flying or of being on a trapeze. The signalman had told me that if I couldn't count twelve between one telegraph pole and another we would be travelling at more than sixty miles an hour. Sometimes the wires were lost behind the tattered sheets of smoke that were blown from the engine and passed our window. I never worked out how fast we were flying.

Beyond the see-sawing telegraph wires the summer sun went on ripening the fields of wheat and barley. The long dykes lowered their water level until their banks looked parched and cracked from want of rain. Flimsy poppies bled on the headlands or gave an oat crop chicken-pox. The railway allotments looked tired and sultry. Runner-beans wilted. Rhubarb leaves as big as elephants' ears hung limp and dull. Hares nibbled at turnip tops and drowsy gate-keepers looked up from their lonely crossings as we thundered by on our way to the sea. Those summers, I tell myself, were days of crisp blue skies and lengthy heatwaves. I took those fen skies and fields for granted, just like the old shepherd. I had no idea that in other parts of the country there were forests or mountains, towns and tall buildings shutting out the sky. My world was seven-eighths sky, as vast as the ocean to which we travelled. Indeed, the sea itself was almost an anti-climax after the pacific cornfields. The sea was nearly always the same colour, but when the wind brushed over this ocean of grain and the sun got caught in the swaying stalks you could see waves of many colours rolling in with shoals of fish flashing beneath the breeze.

Looking back on this cold winter's day to those summers of the mid-thirties I thought I might be guilty of seeing them as I wanted to see them, as weeks of long hot days and warm nights, of dry fields and rainless skies, conveniently forgetting the wet days. But when I consult the weather records of those years I find in fact that we did have some exceptionally good summers then and the low rainfall of 1933 was followed by a long heatwave and drought in 1934.

May, June, July, August. Month after month and year after year the seasons were the same. Life at home and life in the town were the same. There was work and carnivals. School and play. Remembrance Sunday and Sunday School Outings. There was a day when most of the chimneys in our street stopped smoking and a day when the ice-cream man arrived with his donkey and cart. And then, later in the year, there were the days when we re-lit our fires and locked the doors after tea, when we forgot about holidays and huddled together round the hearth in our cramped igloo to tell stories.

November, December, January, February. Another Christmas and another New Year. Some more ice-skating and another birthday. Year after year, celebration after celebration. The same journeys and the same landscape. They haven't changed so very much. The seasons, the festivals

and the landscape are almost the same. I can still sit in a railway compart-
ment and feel the old excitement of travelling, of setting out on a journey.
The years are not separated but held together by the journeys we take.
There is something about the swaying rhythm of the carriage that induces
the mind to travel so many routes.

The journey by rail to March and Ely is one I often prefer to that of
going by road. As you approach the city of Ely you have just about every
aspect of this corner of the fen country in view at one and the same time.
Rich black fields, good crops, reed-beds, the Great Ouse and the great
cathedral itself; the water, sky, land and vegetation, the ancient and
modern history of an important place. Here, in the last few seconds as you
approach the station, is over a thousand years of ecclesiastical, geographical
and social drama. And, being free of a car, it means you can stroll about
more leisurely to look at the city itself as well as the cathedral. Here you
will find historic inns and fine houses, schools and markets, shops and
alleyways that retain much of their original character. It is a city where
you can still get a good meal from a menu of fenland recipes, and where
you can hear great music at some of the concerts held in the cathedral.

I remember being present a year or two ago at a recording of Mahler's
"Resurrection" Symphony with the London Symphony Orchestra, con-
ducted by Leonard Bernstein. Musically and spiritually the experience
was unforgettable. The growing volume of sound under that incredible
lantern tower was inspiring. It was an occasion where, once again, the
way we measure time did not seem to matter. One felt that the building
and the music had been coming together for a thousand years and there,
at that one moment, we gathered to witness their marriage. We had been
privileged to come in from outside and to be part of something that had
no beginning and no end. The stones and the music had been there all the
time. Man shaped the stones into arches and arranged the notes into
harmonies. Their creation took place for us at different times and yet
when we experienced them together that evening they belonged out of
time. When the music dies it will still be forever audible in those stones.
If the stones should fall they will now be forever visible in that music.

When we walked away from the building it was nearly midnight. The
recording session was over. The lights were turned out and the windows
grew dark. Nearby the river flowed on. Beyond the water the fields were
silent. The eight hundred people who had shared that music with us
quickly dispersed and the night breathed deeply with gratitude whilst the
mind vibrated with the glorious sounds it had heard and with the questions always being asked.

Who will know that there was music
in the water and stones?

We have seen the lights flicker
on this symbol of timelessness
and have sounded the depths
of a city's history. The music
was part of our journey,
melodies that haunted the heart,
voices that reached what we called
perfection. But who will know
when the leaves fall and the water
is dull without our reflection
that we ever wept here
in sorrow or pleasure?
When only the stones remain
who will know of our laughter?
If only the music lives on
who will know of these stones?

Early Flooding

The land is still taking a lot of rain and the fields already look hopelessly
waterlogged. It is impossible on some farms to finish lifting the potatoes.
Lorries and machinery get bogged down each day in the sugar-beet fields
and extra tractors have to come to drag them out. The roads are filthy
with mud. The grass verges are now black.

The rivers too are much higher than we would normally expect them
to be this side of Christmas. The Nene is several feet higher and has overflowed the grass on the north bank. The washlands are carrying enough
water at the moment to make it quite easy for swans to land.

Travelling towards Ely again I noticed the washlands between the two
Bedford Rivers completely under water and most of the pasture land was
flooded much sooner in the winter than usual. If this winter is going to be
as hard as many of the local weather-prophets predict, then the threat of
more serious flooding in the spring will be in a lot of people's minds.

Some of these weather-prophets have been extremely accurate before
and put absolute trust in the signs they see in nature; whether it's the
quantity of berries on the hedgerows, or the rabbits and moles burrowing

deeper, or the behaviour of snails and birds, or even the feeling some of them get in their bones. One man told me he only gets warts on his hands when there's going to be a bad winter. This year he has seven warts on his right hand and three on his left. Last year he only had two and he said the only time before in his life when he has had as many as this year was back in 1947. He does not know why this is so, or why the warts disappear again in the spring, but for him it is as reliable as a water-diviner's rod.

When the land is holding so much water it quickly begins to show how close we are to losing all that has been gained over the last few hundred years. Some of the fields that have already been ploughed for winter look more like mud-flats today as the rain stays on the surface. The extra water in the dykes suddenly reminds one again of the complex pattern of water-ways that help to keep this land drained, a remarkable monument to man's efforts to tame this part of England.

The only consolation there will be for some, if these floods stay and the frosts come, will be the chance of getting in some real fenland skating again over acres of ice. There's no need for Bread and Meat Races these days, but skating is so much in the fenmen's blood that they will still hope that if the winter is going to be hard it will be hard enough to give them some pleasure as well as hardship.

Fortunately the rain and the wind eased by the time I was ready to drive home and I travelled back through the early evening's cold light that gave the space a greater emptiness. Darkness grew out of the fields more than the sky and soon the only light on the earth was where the still water in cart-ruts down long droves stared back at the night. The skeleton trees were black. The farm-gates were black and served only to show the official way into each field. They could not keep anyone or anything out. Far off a lamp shines from a farmer's house. He and the dark have come to terms with life, with this haunting solitariness and silent mist. He knows the silence and understands the distances. Wind and rain, summer or winter, his lonely house stands there in a sea of fields that never twice look the same. The house and the owner know all there is to know about the weathers, the seasons, the days and nights of a man's life.

My journey ended, as it always has to end, near the hard lights of the city, where other elements intrude, other voices speak and brasher seasons influence. It is good to shut out the wet night and to sit watching a fire burn with some of the wood we collected in the autumn.

The House with the Blue Shutters

Tonight we went to have dinner with two very good friends who live in Thorney, in a cottage so full of history that several volumes could be written about it, and its owners.

I came to know Hugh and Renate Cave through some of my earlier writings about the fen country and since then their comfortable old cottage has provided me with many enjoyable evenings of talk and memory. To leave the world of darkness and mist and to enter a warm cottage, where the blue shutters so effectively shut out the night, is to move into a world that is both timeless and safe, both harbour and home.

When we arrived this evening the shutters were already folded over the windows and the cottage was quietly lit to underline the atmosphere of peace and relaxation to be found there. I think there are several reasons for this feeling of tranquillity.

The cottage itself is about 300 years old and rests contentedly in the shadows of the ancient abbey. In spring the abbey churchyard is full of snowdrops and the remnants of that once great building can be seen from the front windows. But its shadows and stones were locked out this evening beyond the blue shutters, the world outside and the world inside were separated in just the way we wanted them to be, for we had many years to cover in the next few hours.

Hugh Cave is the most active retired person I know. A man who, after a long career in building and more than thirty years in local government, is still extremely interested in travel, history, education, reading and public service. He has a devotion to his landscape that would be hard to equal. He has also accumulated a considerable collection of family and local history in the weighty files of newspaper articles, photographs, account books and documents that he has taken the trouble to preserve. His wife, Renate, shares his enthusiasms and from her own experience contributes a history which, though quite different, is equally absorbing.

It is not long before we are exchanging memories and anecdotes over an excellent meal which we eat by candlelight. That first hour is but the beginning of a journey into history and local customs that might so easily be forgotten. When we leave the table and go into the lounge which is called 'The Hamburg Room', after Renate's home town, I can see there are several piles of books and papers waiting for me to peruse. . . .

Already I can see from the carefully documented papers that Hugh is showing me that he can trace his family back to 1790, for he has a very detailed family-tree drawn up showing all the marriages, births and deaths from the eighteenth century to the present-day. There are even copies of records that go back a lot farther suggesting that their ancestors can be traced to a Jourdain le Cave, a retainer who came over with William the Conqueror. From the family-tree I turn to a collection of old sepia photographs and then to some leather account books. When I open one of the scrap-books at random I find myself looking at the Apprenticeship Deeds of his great-grandfather—William Cave—dated 1802 in the reign of George III, and start to trace the growth of the family's building firm from that modest beginning to one well-established in the area for the next four generations.

Each file that Hugh produces offers more exciting documents and records that span nearly two hundred years. There are letters from the then Duke of Bedford dated 1879; there are fading photographs of local windmills; copies of Post Office directories from 1830; lists of timber prices and tattered ledgers that belonged to his grandfather and great-grandfather, and details of jobs that would make the modern builder smile.

Some of the prices charged over a hundred years ago make interesting reading and I make a note of some that catch my eye:

1833		£. s. d.
April 29th	Man, 2 days' time on jobs at Congreve's farm, including materials	8. 6.
August 11th	Mending milk stool	6.
1834		
June 29th	Step-ladder, 6′ 6″ long, with block oak etc.	6. 0.
July 16th	Fitting handle to water barrow	2. 0.
1835		
June 27th	Bricklayer and boy, 2 days' time on colouring house	8. 0.
Sept 28th	Ladder, for to reach to clean spouts	1. 2. 0.
1836		
April 30th	Bricklayer, 1 day's time on sundry jobs	3. 0.
Nov 6th	2 Sheep-troughs, 16′ long each	17. 0.

1840		£. s. d.
Dec 20th	3 gallons of tar and tub; new body to wheelbarrow for farm	13. 6.
1844		
May 7th	Mend and paint bee-hive	2. 0.
Oct 23rd	Paint bedroom; paint & time	8. 3½.
1846		
Feb 22nd	Mend old gig; fit new spring and paint	2. 6.
Nov 10th	New spout and mending false bottom for Brewhouse; stuff & time	6. 6.

One page of the account book was to the Overseers of Thorney Parish and consisted mainly of coffins. In 1830 a parish coffin cost twelve and sixpence, plus two and sixpence for taking home, and this price changed very little for the next ten years or so. By 1851 the cost had risen to sixteen shillings and the charge for "taking home" was still only two and sixpence. There are a few exceptional entries, like the one of 1841:

Child's coffin, covered with grey cloth, lined with
white satin; brass breast-plate engraved; silver-
plated furniture: £3. 3. 0d.

And in 1850 there was a special rate charged for a coffin that was made for a farm-labourer killed at work:

for John Delf, killed by a Huddlestone machine
passing over his neck   12. 0d.

The accounts could keep me entertained for quite some while, but I return to reading the Builder's Indenture of 1802, binding the first member of the Cave building family to a five years' apprenticeship:

... during which term the said apprentice his master faithfully shall serve, his secrets keep, his lawful commands everywhere shall gladly do. He shall do no damage to his said master, nor see it to be done of others but to his power shall let or forthwith give warning to his said master of the same. He shall not waste the goods of his said master nor lend them unlawfully to any. He shall not commit fornication, nor contract matrimony within the said term. He shall not play at cards, dice tables, or other unlawful games whereby his said master may have loss. . . . He shall not haunt taverns or playhouses nor absent himself from his said master's services day or night unlawfully but in all things as a faithful servant he shall behave himself. . . .

The master then promises to teach his apprentice all the arts of a carpenter and joiner and to find for the "said apprentice sufficient meat, drink, washing, lodging and all other necessaries during the said term in the consideration of the sum of £10". It is very hard to imagine that any boy of today would be willing to bind himself to such a disciplined apprenticeship.

From the year 1802 I turn to 1914 and pick out an orange-coloured Unemployment Insurance card when the contributions were "five pence per week for a man working more than two days a week, fourpence for a period exceeding one day but not more than two, and twopence for a period not exceeding one day". The card I had in my hand had eleven fivepenny stamps dated 14 January 1914 to 2 October 1914, and for a moment I assumed that the workman had gone off to the war and never returned. But this speculation was a long way out. He simply left his job after a long illness and then went to live in March where he survived to be quite an old man.

Page after page of a very thick scrap-book reveals accounts of floods, festivals, feasts on the green, Coronations and victory celebrations, all part of the life of a village for over a hundred years, a village where generations of the same families still live and still remember.

Hugh tells me about the great blizzard of 1916 when trees were blown down along the Causeway and telegraph poles were brought down near the station.

'My cousin Bill and I were at school in Peterborough and persuaded our teacher to let us leave early so that we could get home before dark and while the trains were still running. As it was, the three o'clock train didn't leave until four and when it finally reached Thorney an hour later it couldn't go any farther. The next train only managed to get within a mile of Thorney station after a two-hour journey and the children had to be carried home by their parents through snow that in places was five feet deep.

'It was 28 March and the extraordinary thing was that the very next day the sun shone as bright as on a summer's day and the snow had nearly all melted by mid-day. The trees and telegraph poles still had to be moved of course and there was a lot of damage to property as well as renewed fears of floods.'

'Where did the local railway line run to then, Wisbech?'

'No, it went as far as Great Yarmouth and was sometimes called "the Crab and Winkle line".

'One of the first companies to operate locally after the 1863 Act was passed was the Peterborough, Wisbech and Sutton Railway but this was later to become The Midland and Great Northern Joint Railway in 1893. The railway carriages were then coffee-coloured and so it wasn't long before they became known locally as "The Coffee-Pot Line". The M & GNJ was just one of the many companies of course to lose its identity with nationalization and Thorney lost its line altogether in 1958.'

Before even the railways came to Thorney the villagers had been used to an earlier form of transport—stage-coaches—and would make their journeys to Peterborough on *The Royal George, The Red Rover,* or *The Wellington.* It was also possible to go by water from Thorney to the Dog-in-a-Doublet and join up with boats operating on the Nene. The boathouse could be seen until just a few years ago but the little river itself has long forgotten that it bore travellers.

Thorney has no lamp-lit railway station now, no coach-houses and no boatmen. Its only links with those romantic days of travel are in the memories of people who, like Hugh Cave, have taken the trouble to preserve some of their history in the files and scrap-books that come alive here more than in any history book. There is such a closeness and authenticity through these fading newspapers and personal documents that the printed pages of even a well-informed book can never quite capture.

From blizzards and railways, stage-coaches and boats, we turn to some articles that are a little more up to date, or I should say that are nearer to our own time. These are cuttings from local papers dated 18 March 1947, reporting on the 100-mile-an-hour gales and the severe floods that happened when the water broke the banks of the River Ouse and the River Welland and overflowed the banks of the Nene. The Great North Road was blocked by fallen trees. Water flowed through the streets of Market Deeping. People sought refuge in their bedrooms as the floods swept through their doors. Boats were out in the streets of Crowland. The Army tried to breach the gaps in the riverbanks with vehicles and sandbags. The main road to Oundle was under three feet of water. Chimneys were snapped off roof-tops, and at Wansford the River Nene was discharging water at the rate of 160 million gallons an hour. Thousands of acres of farmland were drowned and the prospects of summer crops completely ruined.

For a nation only just beginning its recovery from a costly war, from coal-shortages and food-rationing, Nature ought to have shown a little more consideration. But again the men of the fens got to work to re-drain the land and to make it fit for ploughing and sowing. Farmers who had lost cattle started to work out the cost of restocking their farms. Supplies of worms were even imported to help to get the land breathing again.

For a moment my mind leaves the warmth and safety of the cottage and I think of the dark night outside. I can almost feel the damp mist pressing against the walls and the closed shutters. The mist is a permanent reminder that we live in an area at the edge of a world "where neither sea nor land will give in to each other" and where one can never be absolutely sure that we are safe at last.

The abbey clock strikes eleven. The strokes sound muffled and more distant than one would expect from this close proximity. Until the clock spoke I had not thought about time. We had been in this "world within world" with so much of the past that it was difficult to remember even the year, let alone the hour.

The history we have been talking about is nothing, of course, compared with that of Thorney Abbey itself, founded in 662 as a Benedictine monastery. Like the abbey at Crowland, and those at Ely and Peterborough, it was raided and destroyed by the Danes in 870, its wooden buildings burnt to the ground and many of its monks murdered. But it was rebuilt in 972 and during the next two or three centuries established an impressive and wealthy church with several farms, vineyards and considerable lands in Cambridgeshire and Lincolnshire. It remained so until the Dissolution when the stone building was again ransacked, the lead roof was taken off and the carved woodwork of the screen and choir stalls thrown on to the fire. For a time all life at Thorney appears to have come to an end. The land was left uncultivated. The vineyards disappeared. The ruins left open to the wet fen weather. During the reign of Edward VI much of the original building was so badly broken down that nearly two hundred tons of stone were given to the University of Cambridge for building work at Trinity and Corpus Christi Colleges. There was little left of the magnificent building that was once five times its present size and which rivalled its fenland neighbours. The little that was left was eventually restored in the seventeenth century by the Duke of Bedford and this became the parish church, which was also to have quite a remarkable history during the next three hundred years.

In 1640 Bishop Wren granted a licence to Stephen de Cursal to preach at Thorney in French and Latin so that the French Huguenots, who had been forced to seek refuge, first in Holland and then in England, could hold their own services in the new church there. Most of the Huguenots who came to Thorney had been helping with drainage work in the Isle of Axeholme or had tried to settle in Doncaster. But they were not given a very warm welcome in Yorkshire where their homes and families were constantly attacked. They were not allowed to work or live for themselves and for a time England appeared to be no safer for them than France, or Holland, where they had been pursued and persecuted for their religious beliefs. Their brief stay in Holland had at least taught them how to drain and farm the lowlands—knowledge which was certainly in their favour when life became unbearable for them in Yorkshire and they had the chance of moving into the fens.

When they heard that the Earl of Bedford had some partly reclaimed land at Thorney in Cambridgeshire, they asked if they might rent it and try to cultivate it. Permission was granted, and more than fifty families moved from Yorkshire to begin what was to be an important period of drainage and agriculture.

One of their first crops was colza—something like a wild cabbage—from which they could also extract the oil they needed for their lamps. Corn soon became another successful crop, and they also learnt how to grow and mill the woad still used in this country for dyeing wool.

Through the fourth Earl of Bedford the French settlers at Thorney were later granted other privileges by Charles II, including the right to hold religious services in the abbey church every Sunday at times alternating with the services in English. Their first pastor was the Reverend Father Ezekiel Danois, who began his ministry in Thorney in 1642 and who, during the next twenty-two years, did a great deal to establish and organize the life of his community, encouraging learning and reading among his people. But although the Reverend Danois was allowed to preach in French and to baptize the children of the Huguenot families, he was not permitted to marry them, bury them, or conduct the Holy Communion service. These services had to be performed in English by the abbey's own parson; even so, by the end of the seventeenth century as many as five hundred communicants were receiving the sacraments.

So the "Isle of Thorns", that in the twelfth century had been so prosperous with its vineyards, sheep and fruit trees, was to grow again out of the wasteland of its neglect to become, by the middle of the seventeenth century, an island in the fens, that was both favoured and fair—as it has been ever since. It is interesting, too, to remember how many different nationalities went into that new prosperity and achievement—French, Dutch, Irish and English being some of the larger contingents.

More recently permission has been given for the Roman Catholics of Thorney to hold Mass in the abbey—the first time in over four hundred years that a Catholic service has been held in an Anglican church.

Before the Catholics of Thorney were allowed to use the abbey they met for "House Mass" in the cottage where I now sat going through a family's history; and I could see now another reason for the feeling of tranquillity experienced in this room. People had gathered here once a month from 1968 to 1974, to continue and preserve their faith in their own village as well as attending the Catholic Church in Peterborough. Hugh Cave himself comes from a devout family of Catholics which he knows goes back to the parents of his great-grandmother, Mary McGuire, in the late 1770s.

It is interesting that Thorney should have accommodated so amicably religions that in themselves have histories of conflict. But then, this village has always been a home for people seeking refuge, tolerance and hospitality. The Huguenots were certainly able to settle down here better than in Yorkshire and they stayed long enough to become a thriving community. The Irish immigrants too, who came over in the middle of the eighteenth century, were given permission to live together and the Duke of Bedford built the "Ave Maria Cottages" for them at Thorney Toll. More recently, during the First World War, Belgian refugees also came to Thorney and today people from other parts of the country still come to find their own retreat in this fair and ancient "island".

Renate has been showing Mary Edmunds, their other guest for the evening, the history that she is compiling from her own articles, photographs and events. Thorney is, for Renate, a long way from her home town in Germany but it has become "home", and she takes a keen and active interest in the life of the village as well as in the history of the fens, supporting adult education classes, local concerts and the Women's Institute.

The day ends as the abbey clock strikes midnight and we remember that there is still a journey of seven miles to make, perhaps through a thick fog. But once again it is difficult to end a conversation that has really only just begun. How can you condense five hundred years into five hours? So, although we move to the hall and put on our coats, the stories continue a little longer. We hear a few more local legends, such as Ashley's Pool being known as "Medicine Pond" because long ago a doctor always prescribed the same bottles of greeny-coloured medicine, whatever the illness, making his patients think that the contents were no more than the stagnant water from Ashley's Pool. The pool is also supposed to be the grave of a coach and two (or was it four?) horses that left the road one foggy night long ago. Some of the older residents may even assure you that ghosts have been seen to rise from the pond on such a night as this, so we were grateful that we didn't have to take that particular road home. When we eventually left the house with the blue shutters we did not see any phantoms, ghosts or skeletons, not even from the abbey churchyard where so much past lay buried. In fact the mist had cleared slightly and a few stars glimmered like distant lighthouses in the sky between the rocky clouds. As we made our way home along the Causeway we knew that we would have to go back soon to continue the conversation we had been unable to complete in one evening. This leave-taking was not an end but a beginning.

Origins

Following the stories of last night I spent the morning looking at old maps of the area and have come to understand a little more the origins of some of the place names that exist in the fens. And there are some very unusual and intriguing names too—Teakettle Hall, Rogue's Alley, Botany Bay, Whipchicken Farm, Hangman's Corner, Hollow Heap, Beggar's Bridge, Creekgall Fen, Eternity Hall, White Fen and Powder Blue Farm. Many have a ring of the Wild West about them, others take their names from incidents that are now lost to history. Some preserve all that is left of a part of history, and all must have been given their names for a reason.

Powder Blue Farm is an example, and on the face of it, would appear to be the most untypical name to give to a farm in the black fen country. Its name takes us back again to the days when woad was used in this country as a dye. The woad was a plant that was grown in abundance at one time in the fens and continued to be used long after those early Britons had abandoned the idea of painting their bodies. In fact woad was grown in this area until late in the eighteenth century, and the last woad mill in England was pulled down at Parson Drove in 1914. When the plant had been harvested and dried it was then ground into a fine powder which was then resoaked and allowed to ferment for several months. It wasn't the most pleasant of smells that pervaded the air and must have made as many noses twitch as the smell of refining sugar-beet does today. The substance that was left after fermentation was then strained and rolled into balls ready for selling as dyes, mainly to the clothing trade. Examples of the process can still be seen in the museum in Wisbech.

But why Powder Blue Farm? We find the answer among the Huguenots who came to settle in the Thorney district. Because the making of woad dye was an unpleasant job it was left very much to the Frenchmen and their descendants who became some of the main growers and millers. For them the blue powder would have been called *poudre bleu* and this was the name they presumably gave to one of their farms. Three hundred years after their arrival in this country and long after the disappearance of woad they are still remembered in such names as Powder Blue Farm, French Farm and French Drove.

The more I think about the mass of material that I was able to handle last night at Hugh Cave's house the more convinced I am that there must be hoards of documents and old papers hidden away in some of those old farms with unusual names—secrets that will never be told, stories that will never be heard, articles that will be thrown away because, as people so often say, 'I never thought they'd be of interest to anybody.'

A person, though, who does know that her connections with the fens go back for at least three hundred and fifty years is Mrs Jean Gill, whose French ancestors joined the Thorney community in 1659, having already lived in this country for six or seven years, most possibly with those Protestant refugees who had tried unsuccessfully to settle in Yorkshire before moving south.

Mrs Gill's determination to find the proof she needed turned out to be quite a detective story itself; and, once again, a chance remark—an accident or coincidence, call it what you will—started her off in her own pursuit of her family's origins. Being told one day that because of her demonstrative hands she must have French blood in her veins she began a long sequence of inquiries that were to lead her eventually, not only to Thorney, Gedney and Fleet in Lincolnshire, but also to Valenciennes and Artois on the Continent, to a five-hundred-year-old heritage and a family-crest with the motto *Tant S'en Faut.*

Her luck turned when she was able to read a very rare publication called *A Genealogical Memoranda Relating to the Huguenot Family of de Vantier, anglais Wanty, of Thorney.* This document, collected and arranged by Henry Peet FSA of Liverpool, in 1902, gave Mrs Gill the most positive clue to work on, for in its pages were names that were to mean a lot to

It could not have been worse,
the sky so full of vengeance,
the day so drenched with rain
it did not matter which was
heaven or earth. The wind
blew with a knife's pain
so that the winter grass
raced for the safety of low dykes . . .

her during the next few months as, piece by piece, she slowly established her family tree.

The history of the Wanty family went beyond Thorney once the people had settled down in their new country. They were industrious workers and soon began to farm land in other parts of the district, particularly at Gedney and Fleet, where Mrs Gill's own grandfather and father had farmed and where she had spent her own childhood, a childhood that she remembers now was not without stories of ghosts, suspicions, fortunes, speculations and eccentric relations. Was it true there was buried treasure somewhere near the house where she had lived? Was it possible that she had French blood in her veins? Were her features and mannerisms more continental than Anglo-Saxon? Could the growing "homesickness" for the Continent be a long buried desire to go back home, to return to those long-ago villages from which her ancestors had come?

Mrs Gill admitted to me in our conversation that she was not a lover of the fens at all, nor of the fenland character which can be so dour and reserved. She didn't like people who played their cards too close to their chest, she said, but preferred the warmth and liberality, the easy and out-going generosity she found in people across the Channel. This feeling of having no real, deeply-rooted loyalty to the fens also encouraged her to find where "her roots" were.

Eventually, through a detailed study of Mr Peet's chronicle, a family-tree was established that not only satisfied her but was also officially approved and recognized as the authentic "Pedigree of the Wanty Family", commencing with Abraham de Vantier and Marie Cherbeau and continuing down to the present day and Mrs Gill's own children. From those first Vantiers (now Wantys) can be traced a direct line of descendants, the family name changing when Sarah Ann Wanty married James Benson, from which parentage Mrs Gill's mother came and to which future generations, it is hoped, will belong.

Several other members of the Wanty family sailed for America in the eighteenth and nineteenth centuries and were to achieve distinction in the world of law and politics, a remarkable record of a family's enforced dispersal and then success from those original refugees who left their native land in the hope of saving their own family.

Having established this much about the origins of her own demonstrative hands and dark eyes Mrs Gill's next hope is that she can link up with some of the remaining offspring of those relatives who, at the moment, are only names and strangers on a sheet of paper. Then, with her own compass-needle pointing more and more towards Europe, she would like to leave these low, damp regions of the fens for somewhere with more sun and security, somewhere with a greater sense of belonging. 'It's a long time to be away from home,' she said, 'and now I have discovered this much I know I shall only be happy when the exile is over. . . . I suppose some people will think I'm sentimental but when *you* talk about this landscape and what it means to you perhaps you can understand what it is I am trying to say.'

Castle Rising

Today I went out again into Marshland, to the waiting silence and the emptiness. Any signs of life there were could hardly be discerned. They were as sparse and as inconspicuous as the few drops of water left in a fine glass from which the liquid has been drained.

The roads that go as near as they dare to the land's edge, or the sea's beginning, were as desolate as if no one had travelled on them for a hundred years. Beyond Terrington St Clement and Clenchwarton they reach out into a no-man's-land, a land of reeds, birds, low winds and mist.

Today the air was clear but cold, too cold to stand on that exposed plateau for very long. In the distance the sea looked slate grey. The light on the marshes was golden and glistening. Golden on the frayed banners of sedge. Glistening on the wet, muddy creeks.

To cross the River Ouse, and to continue my journey into Norfolk, I had to go into King's Lynn again before I could get back on to quieter roads, roads that draw you quickly away from the busy crowds and out into the small villages and country lanes. There the four-wheels can be discarded once more and the legs stride out into a landscape where cars cannot get.

Finding that the wind was still giving away millions of free razor-blades I was glad to seek the shelter of the car though after a brief walk. My face tingled with a thousand tiny, invisible cuts and my ears felt as if they were frost-bitten. The marshes may have beckoned and I would have liked longer on them, but I convinced myself that the wind was too cold and so I returned to North Wootton and Castle Rising where I was able to visit again the castle ruins and the ancient almshouses, or—to give them their correct title—The Hospital of the Most Holy and Undivided Trinity.

This building was not a hospital in the modern sense of the word but a place of refuge for aged and single ladies who could no longer find a home in the remaining convents. They had to be "of honest life and conversation, religious, grave and discreet . . . fifty-six years of age at least, no common beggar, harlot, scold, drunkard or haunter of taverns". The hospital was built by the benevolent Henry Howard, Earl of Northampton, who lived from 1540 to 1614, and it is a splendid example of early seventeenth-century planning and brickwork. Little has changed. Electricity and central heating may have been introduced and some of the residents' rooms may have television, but the entrance gate, the courtyard, the dining hall and the chapel can all be seen as they were originally designed. And there is still an atmosphere of tranquillity there in this quiet corner of Norfolk, perhaps more tranquil now than it was in those days when the hospital's heavy doors had to be shut early every evening and not opened again until daylight, when an upstairs room housed a valuable treasury chest and when King's Lynn was still an easy hide-out for rogues and robbers. The room with its original Jacobean panelling and the Treasury Chest can be seen on request and it is worth spending a few minutes up in that part of the building where the local council felt their safety guaranteed.

There was a time when Castle Rising was even more important than Lynn, which hardly existed, when Rising was a prosperous seaport. That was when it stood on the then tidal river of Babingley and ships could navigate their way up to its quaysides. An old rhyme survives that tells of the changing fortunes of these neighbours:

> Rising was a seaport town
> When Lynn was but a marsh.
> Now Lynn it is a seaport town
> And Rising fares the worse.

This takes the history of Castle Rising back for over a thousand years for Lynn's popularity as a port goes back almost that long. Indeed, there was a time when Rising was a Borough with its own Mayor and two Members of Parliament, one was the diarist Samuel Pepys and the other was Sir Robert Walpole.

The importance of Rising though can still be imagined from the impressive fortification built in 1150 during the reign of King Stephen, and it must have been a castle that had many fine architectural beauties, including a magnificent stone stairway that rises steeply through a sequence of perfectly proportioned arches.

It was here that Edward III imprisoned his mother Isabella for her part in the murder of his father Edward II in 1327. She died in her room in 1358.

From the high windows of the ruins today you look out over the peaceful village, over a pattern of beautiful red rooftiles on the barns and houses, and in the distance you can see Wootton marshes fading into the sea.

If the wind had blown cold down on those marshes it blew even colder now up on the ruined walls on this hill. It came from the north and brought with it the chill of snow and the abrasive saltiness of the sea. The marshes look particularly desolate and uninviting from this distance. They also look mockingly triumphant.

To the south, where pine trees and woodlands offer protection, is Sandringham House with its gardens, lawns, meadows, rhododendrons and church, approached by travelling through some of the finest avenues of trees in the country. It is difficult to believe that such a rich estate is so near to the solitary landscape of marsh and fen.

There is nothing solitary about Sandringham now, not even when the Royal family is absent, for it has become a very popular place for tourists in cars and in coaches who arrive in their hundreds during the summer and at most week-ends throughout the year. Several of the loveliest roads that used to be private have now been opened to the public and there are picnic areas beneath the trees.

I stayed in Norfolk until the late afternoon light began to fade and rain clouds came stampeding in over the sea completely spoiling any prospect of a good sunset. So I turned for home and drove back to King's Lynn, Wisbech and Thorney.

Next to a good book, I think an atlas is the most absorbing piece of reading to have on a winter's evening. Within minutes the mind has packed its bags and is off on routes that go over land that may never be travelled in reality but still give the excitement of discovery. It need not be a quick journey, tracing the finger along red lines at seventy miles an hour. Cross-roads have histories. The names of places, as I've found out, have their legends. Small shaded areas are towns or villages where people live, people I shall never meet yet feel I know. Dots are farms where lights and fires burn and where other men plan their seasons. I listen to the atlas and in the silence of the night I hear many voices.

A Hard Land

There are times when it is difficult to praise, or to willingly be part of, this landscape. There are times when it mocks and ridicules, when it offends and rejects so totally that one wonders how such a love for it has ever endured or been real before. For days now it has been so hostile and so ruthless that the spirit eventually gives in and shares the depression.

Today is even colder and greyer, windier and wilder than it has been so far all winter. The cold penetrates in a way that chills the blood and gnaws at the stomach's muscles. It is such a dry, arid cold. The north-easterly wind comes with a Siberian accent, day after day, until every brick of the house aches with cold. We try shutting out the draughts but the bitter air eats through everything.

I sit looking out of the window. The sky is ice-grey. The bare trees and the stubs of rose bushes shiver in the wind. For a few moments the wind tears itself on the rose thorns and screams with pain. It bangs its fists on the windows and spits on the glass. But those few splashes of icy rain do not sweeten or soften the earth at all. The soil is hard and cracked. As lifeless as a desert. It's impossible to believe that beneath that dull crust the bulbs of crocuses, snowdrops, daffodils and tulips are already timing their birth, already preparing for the announcement of spring.

The sky that has known so many exciting days of cloud and sunshine this year is now a flat, frozen, grey, solid canvas on which no other shade is seen. There is dust in the wind. Cold, lifeless dust. And the monotony and the persistence of the wind under such greyness chills the spirit into submission. There are no words left to describe the grimness of the cold. It comes like an awful plague to the streets and the houses. I turn away from the window and draw up a chair to the fire and stare at the flames. But even the flames look cold and the wind jeers down the chimney. The cold wind always wins. All the elements win in their own time. The sea, the mist, the sun and the wind, fire and frost, gales and floods, all win when they want to win. We can offer resistance and hold them back when they are only half determined to defeat us. But when it is their turn to win we are usually powerless.

Restless, and unable to work this morning, I go back to looking out of the window on to the garden. There is a blue-tit swinging on the string of monkey-nuts that I have looped round the bird-table. They are comical little birds at times. They do the most irrational things. They are scatter-brained and grasshopper-minded. Or so it would appear. For instance the one I am watching now has landed on the rose bush nearest to the table and has selected which nut he is going to go for. He flits to the loop of nuts and begins pecking away for several seconds, sparks of monkey-nut shell flying off in all directions. Then, just when the nut is visible, he hops along the string to another nut that has not been started and begins pecking away again. He does this about four times and just when I think he is going to take a nut he flies off and disappears. Some minutes later another tit, a fatter, bossy-looking tit, arrives and goes straight to one of the red nuts, picks it out and flies off into a nearby tree where it starts eating the meal the other poor little chap had worked for so hard. Is there a social system in the tit family that decrees who shall work and who shall eat, I wonder? Was the first tit only meant to "peel the potatoes" ready for the second tit to dine?

At least it was a diversion. It took my mind off the greyness of the day and the cold sky. What about being out in the fields now, I think to my-self, where the wind is even more merciless and where you would have cause to complain. And my mind goes back to a winter or two ago when I walked along the headlands with a man who had spent many winters in such unkind conditions. That was when I began to change my romantic view of being a land-worker:

> I would have portrayed you once
> as part of the rich character
> of these fields, your ponderous limp
> a product of the black soil, the split
> roots of your hands wealthy as muck.
>
> I would have dressed you in words
> to keep out the raw winds of your life,
> would have made you spectacular
> as the sun rising in winter, or as part
> of a landscape by Breughel the elder.
>
> But that would have gilded
> your rank flower, would have disguised
> the exhausted bud of your eyes
> and silenced the loud ache
> of your bones' arthritis.

For someone's gain you have banged
your head on a sky of indifference.
You have grown old cursing the fields
for survival—a by-product of wealth
defying description.

The fire does not look cold any more. The room is a generous comfort.

Winter Dark

Darkness comes with four o'clock and the day is over by the time we make an afternoon cup of tea. I have not been out of the house all day and feel as if I have been imprisoned for weeks. The nearest field feels a hundred miles away. I cannot work. My eyes ache for distance.

And now it is too late. The sky has shut itself away behind the night. The distance is locked behind the silence. The stars too are absent. All I can do now is go for a walk round the neighbouring streets and the nearby park. But there will at least be space in the darkness.

Empty streets on winter evenings present their own kind of solitary landscape. Lights are on in the houses, yellow squares that nearly always look alike and yet hide so many differences.

I look down one street of winter-lit houses and notice the pattern of lights and locked doors. The houses have been there for over a hundred years. The families have come and gone, but each winter the curtains are drawn, the lights are switched on, the doors are locked against the darkness. There's a feeling of constancy in such a simple ritual. The lighted windows have such a silent eloquence, a language that is always waiting to be deciphered in the cold, lonely street.

For a moment I feel a stranger in my own town. I feel as if I have stopped somewhere in an unknown place. As if I have stepped back a hundred years. No one else walks the pavements. No cars turn into the street or pull up at one of the houses. It remains silent and empty for several minutes; silent and strange until, from the far end of the street, I hear the first carol-singers of the year.

I feel my ears prick up like those of a dog. I wait and listen. They are the usual, familiar, out-of-key carols that have been sung each year at those front doors for a century. The same nervous beginnings, the same jumble of half-forgotten words, the same haste to get through enough verses to justify knocking on the door.

"Away in a Manger" is back with us again and boys who, during the rest of the year, have been singing more raucous songs or screaming at football matches are once more trying to achieve a degree of angelic innocence and love of babies that will impress the people on the other sides of the doors.

Hearing this first untuneful carol of the winter makes me feel happy and reminds me that we are rapidly approaching the season loathed and loved by nearly everyone. We must love it otherwise we would not be so willingly caught up in all its arrangements and celebrations. But the preparation and the extravagance, the expectations and the competition, all this conflicts with what could be pure joy.

Certainly the carol takes my mind back again to my childhood when we went out carolling with paraffin lamps and torches to light our way and hot potatoes in our pockets to keep us warm. I *think* we had more fun then. I'm sure we sang the carols better and gave our customers a few verses for their money. To begin with most of us went to Sunday School so knew the verses and, of course, we knew the people who lived in those houses more than the children can today. Some families shared the same streets for generations, even the same houses. The house in which I was born had been the home of my great-grandparents. There was a continuity that helps confidence.

The youngsters braving the cold streets for the first time this year quickly make their breathless way from house to house, knocking knockers and ringing bells after just a few lines before moving on to the next house. Perhaps they hear the televisions inside being turned up to a louder volume that drowns their own efforts. Perhaps they suddenly remember who lives there and their "Angels from the realms of glory" get lost in frightened giggles as they scamper across the road to try the houses opposite.

I move on too and walk into the shopping centre which looks its best at night with all the shops closed and the traffic gone. If I'd looked at the shop windows more carefully the last time I was in town I would have known that Christmas was getting near, for I see them now full of expensive gifts, decorations, cards, fruit, nuts, wine, turkeys, jewellery, gaudy trinkets, baubles and festive trivia that gives commerce its last big chance of cashing-in on the season of good-will before the deep depression that is also promised arrives, starless and kingless.

The desperation of last-minute buyers is yet to strip these displays, leaving the shops in ruins until the January sales of the New Year that will surely come, and so now, in the silence of the after-shopping hours,

I gaze at windows that for a few more days will convince us of prosperity and generous thoughts. I even feel excited to realize that Christmas is only a week or so away.

The walk has done me good. I feel lighter than I did earlier in the day and begin to make out a list of Christmas presents and cards. I also begin to look forward most of all to Christmas Eve for it is then that I still find the season has some magic, some moment that will make each and all of Christmas worthwhile. Sometimes it has been a quiet Christmas Eve dinner at a small hotel with friends. Sometimes it has been at a simple service in a local church. Sometimes it has been a moment on television when, back home and nearing midnight, we have sat and watched a programme of carols from King's College Chapel choir, or it has been a lonely walk out in the fens under a cold, crispy star-lit sky when one looked up and expected one star brighter than the rest. . . .

I think particularly now of one such Christmas Eve when I had been out walking and came home to give the first presents and to raise the first festive glass. A good fire was burning. The room was warm and looked plentiful with its bowls of fruit and nuts, its walls draped with greetings-cards and the coloured candles lit. Slowly we unwrapped the paper from the new books or records (seldom a tie or a shirt) and then we switched on the television to watch a carol service from Lincoln cathedral. The camera reached along the pillars as if looking for the sound and the first phrase we heard came from two young choristers singing, unaccompanied, "In the bleak mid-winter...". Their clear, pure voices echoed through the choir stalls and under the roof. And suddenly the simplicity and the majesty, the history and the meaning, were all drawn together in that moment. How they achieved such innocence only their mothers will know. For us it set the seal on a Christmas Eve that would have compelled not only Thomas Hardy to go again into the stable's gloom "hoping it might be so". It meant something that went beyond the event that the occasion was all about... or perhaps I really mean it caught, for that moment, what the celebration *was* all about, stripped of its trimmings and extravagance.

I hope it will be so again in a week's time.

I

Now

Not a star moves out of place. Orion is as constant in its distance and form as it has been since Man gave names to constellations. The air is clear enough for us to see the Pleiades and nearer reaches of the Milky Way. The sky is silent. No hint of echoes from beyond the space that separates the stars. On earth the fields are dark with darker shapes of trees. And village lights, like stars caught in the grass, give meaning to the miles we travel through.

The city is left behind. We pass the villages of Orton Longueville, Orton Waterville, Alwalton and Chesterton. In the distance is Fotheringhay and its royal church. We cannot see it but we know it's there. It's all part of the history we feel on roads that knew a certain tragedy or fame four centuries ago. We mention every village tucked between those spaces on the earth and hidden now beyond the waiting dark. It's all so familiar. The earth and sky. And yet tonight it has this annual significance when out of the fixed and ordinary things we look for miracles. If a star did move, if sounds were to come from the sky, we'd tremble and be terrified. But because nothing unusual happens we drive on in a world of our own towards the ancient town of Oundle and The Talbot Hotel for our Christmas Eve dinner.

Arriving out of the country dark into the brightness of the town the lights hurt our eyes, the streets bring us back to reality. Cars are parked outside the hotel. The bars are crowded. The inn, appropriately, is full. The dining-room is warm and candle-lit. Tables steam with good food. Glasses glow with wine. Surely the statisticians can't be right about half the world starving! Not on Christmas Eve? So who's got it wrong?

The conscience is consoled by words like, 'But what can you do about it now? After all, you're not making a pig of yourself.' No, but the thought was there, as uncomfortable as a stab of indigestion half-way through the second course. And only our wish to be quiet on Christmas Eve and away from all the last-minute panic in the city redeems the deed. Here, in a public place, it is surprisingly easy to be private and alone, to find the time to ponder over some of the values and memories. To feel gratitude and contentment.

We drive back through the silent countryside—Southwick, Woodnewton, Nassington, Wansford, Southorpe and Ufford. The roads twist between hedges and stone walls, past cottages and rooms where children sleep with presents now at the foot of their beds. On this one night of the year it all has to be true. . . .

The villages wait. The fields remain dark. And not a star moves out of place. Not a sound comes from the sky.

As It Was

After a quiet Christmas Eve I still have what is, I suppose, an old-fashioned Christmas, spending Christmas Day at the home of my parents with other members of the family. Sometimes there can be fourteen of us gathered round the table and each year the same games are played, the same stories told, the same memories brought out like the carols, decorations and nut-crackers to give the season its customary pattern. And always other Christmasses come back into our thoughts and conversations. When I watch my six-year-old nephew, David, I see quite clearly those Christmas Days I had when I was a child his age. The mystery of the old man with a red cloak and a white beard who somehow squeezed down our chimney with a sack of toys ceased to be a mystery in the morning when the bottom of the bed was loaded with presents. The thrill of waking early and rushing into my parents' bedroom with some of the toys, the excitement of going downstairs into a room that had been transformed during the night with a Christmas tree and coloured lights, the very taste of the home-made pork pie we had for breakfast, all come back to me as I see myself in this other child. . . .

By the time breakfast was over the day was really alive. The radio would be loud with "Christians Awake" or "O Come all ye faithful" and final preparations for our Christmas Dinner would put the small kitchen out of bounds as far as the children were concerned. Toy cannons shot down a troop of cavalrymen, a new fire-engine crashed into the piano, and happy shouts came from every part of the house. Into this confusion of noise, colour, crackers, balloons and humming-tops came my grandparents to spend their Christmas quietly with us.

No one bothered how much coal or wood was put on the fire. The room just grew hotter and hotter. One year the paper decorations caught fire and all the balloons burst. There was a great fanning of arms and towels and stamping of feet. The room filled with a grey cloud of smoke that spread into a black snowstorm and I rushed out into the yard shouting

'Fire! Fire!'. There was no one to hear me. The neighbours were in-
volved in their own fires. The forlorn white world outside looked cold and
desolate. Only the birds had life as they pecked away at a few scraps that
had been thrown out for them. They did not even look up as I waved my
arms in an abortive attempt to raise the alarm. The sky was as expression-
less as a frozen pond. The old wash-house at the bottom of the garden
looked far away and forsaken. The water-tap was frozen and a long icicle
hung there gnarled and white as candle-wax.

When my mother called me back into the house the panic was over.
The smoke was disappearing through the open window and I could see
quite clearly now the unperturbed outlines of the china dogs on the
mantelpiece and the untroubled face of the wall clock. From the ceiling
hung the wire skeletons of Chinese lanterns and the charred pieces of tape
on which the balloons had blossomed.

'Would you like a game of draughts?' asked my grandmother, as if
nothing had happened, 'or Snakes and Ladders?'

This question made the fire only the beginning of the afternoon's fun
or drama. The shake of the dice or the appearance of the cards or draught-
board fanned flames that were just as dangerous, for my grandmother
never liked to lose. If she saw that this was likely to happen she would
accuse us all of cheating and throw the board up into the air so that no one
could win.

Sometimes my grandparents would stay all day and sometimes they
would leave later in the afternoon to have tea with one of my aunts. When
they stayed all day some of my aunts, uncles and cousins would come to
spend their evenings with us as well. Then the fun was four-fold and the
events would be quite unpredictable. The table—a big round table that
stood permanently in the centre of the room—would be cleared for cards,
dominoes, or "tippet" and the door to the stairs would be closed to take
the dartboard. There would be singing and laughter and stories of local
characters who haunted our Christmasses then like ghosts of long ago. If
half the stories were true then no town has ever had more clowns,
lunatics, drunks or eccentrics than ours.

I heard of strange old characters in the fens who were laws unto themselves—men who never washed from one year's end to another, who
worked stripped to the waist even in winter and who wrestled with bulls
for shilling bets. One uncle told a murder story while another uncle sang
"Ten Green Bottles". I heard about the days when the King's Dyke
Silver Prize Band went out carol-playing in snow so deep they lost their
euphonium-player and how Flowery George tripped over his lantern and

rolled into a ditch that extinguished them both. The same characters were talked about each year, characters whose idiosyncrasies earned them a place in the folk-lore of the town and won for them an affection that has been handed down from one generation to the next; characters who could turn a simple phrase into something quite extraordinary and memorable, such as "I remember the first time I went up a ladder was down a well", or "Without a word of a lie I know that's true 'cus I stood at my clock as the door struck twelve".

The family laughed as they laughed each year and one story prompted another so that in the end everyone had recalled some favourite character. There was Billy Blunt and Rowdy Dick the drover, Porky Frost and Charlie Smack.

'The night I shall never forget,' I heard someone say, 'was that winter when we piled snow right up above Billy Cuckoo's front door and windows and then dropped a bottle down the chimney with a message in it which said THE END IS NEAR. They reckon he was still praying when they dug 'im out three days later.'

'What about the night when old Rowdy Dick drove his bullocks into the police station to report them for being drunk and disorderly. . . .'

'What about that time when Uncle 'Lijah came to stay and was still sober after eighteen pints. . . .'

'What about that trouble we had. . . . Trouble? There's always been trouble in this town. . . . Do you remember the Whittlesey Riots?'

The voices fell over themselves to get their memories in first and I heard about a time when the people of the town started a brief but wild rebellion because they were not going to receive their customary supply of firewood from the polling booths used at the General Election. I heard that in those days the only polling station was on the market square where several wooden booths were erected for voting and then, at the end of the day, these were broken up and given to the poor. When this concession was taken away from them the townspeople grew angry, pulled up the cobbles that covered the square and went round the town smashing the windows of shops and also those of the local officials they held responsible for the new order. My grandmother said she could definitely remember the women using their aprons to hold the cobbles dug out by the men and how they went running down Market Street with their ammunition.

The fen-country has always had its share of trouble and rioting, enough to prove that when the fenman's passions are roused he is far from the sullen, docile creature he may appear on the surface. The riots at Ely, Littleport, Upware and Southery are famous accounts of what happens

when he loses his temper. The minor uprisings of other towns too have
not been without violence. It is a stubborn temper which, like high-water
in the fens, is only just kept in check. When the banks break the conse-
quences are usually disastrous.

. . . My nephew and his sister, Karen, become bored with their new
toys and say, 'I know, let's make a play. You be Red Riding Hood and
I'll be the wolf.' And so the years and memories are lost in an hour of
dramatizing the fairy stories that amuse them more than their toys or the
television show. They mimic and make up lines as they go. They make
costumes out of an assortment of scarves and build palaces out of old
cardboard boxes. We act some of the plays three times over, each playing
the different characters in turn. Into this confusion of noise, colour,
crackers and balloons, *their* grand-parents came to spend a Christmas
quietly with them.

New Year

The calendar tells me that the year is over only to begin again after midnight on the first day of the first month when we shall expect miracles
again or make promises which will soon be broken.

But with half of winter still to come I can't see the first day of January
as the beginning of the year. I think the new year ought to start in spring.
Let the grey and wrinkled days of January and February belong to winter
and the old year. Let us make our new resolutions when the bright flowers
appear, when the days lengthen and light returns to the land. Why start
a new year in semi-darkness, in frost or snow or floods?

But the calendars have been designed, published, bought and given and
so tonight the last pin-up or country-scene will be taken down to make
way for another collection of dreams. A few million people will go to
parties to keep the tradition alive. A few more million will go to bed at
their usual times knowing that no amount of bell-ringing, first-footing or
glass-waving will change their luck. A few people who still believe in
fortune will leave some money out of doors tonight and fetch it in again
on New Year's morn. If it is still there (and they usually put it where no
one will find it) they then know they will not go without during the next
twelve months.

I think it's reassuring that dark men, lumps of coal and lucky coins still
mean something in a welfare state. They may not delay the coming of a

new Ice Age by one minute but they belong to our dark past that may
have been lost in an old Ice Age. Our superstitions go back such a long way
that to indulge in them now, when we have so many reliable safeguards
against extreme poverty or fate, is to acknowledge a link with those
ancient forefathers that is basic and perhaps, in the end, indestructible.

I welcome in the New Year for the simple reason it would be in-
consistent to go to bed before midnight on this one night of the year when
I never do on any other. Being a nocturnal creature I seldom think of
sleep before the early hours of the morning, so why not open the doors
and listen to the ringing bells? Why not put some money out where no
one will find it? Why not enjoy this special midnight and refill the glass?

The morning arrives without a hangover, but because it is New Year's
Day I feel more like walking than working (which is not a good beginning)
and so I go out once more to the usual starting point by the River Nene.

The first thing I notice as I climb over the gate to walk along the eastern
side of the bridge is a line of dead moles hanging from a barbed-wire
fence. It is a fairly common sight in the fens but one that always has a
touch of the macabre about it. The moles have to be trapped and killed,
not only in the fields but also along the riverbanks, for they can cause
hundreds of pounds' worth of damage. But why they have to be strung up
for exhibition like this I don't know. I'm told it's to show the farmer, or
the drainage officers, that the mole-catcher has done his job well. I'm told
that it's always been a tradition among mole-catchers to hang the dead
moles on the land from which they were taken. But a line of thirty-seven
little black corpses staring at you early on New Year's Day is a stomach-
turning experience. We may not be as civilized as we'd like but we are
sufficiently removed from public-hangings and human heads on stakes to
recognize other degrees of barbarity. I wouldn't have thought it was
necessary these days to turn the dead moles into some chilling kind of
abacus to count how many victims there'd been. I put this to a mole-
catcher recently and he replied, 'Every man has a right to take a pride in
his work.'

I look at the thirty-seven on the fence near the gate. Their furs are still
new, their shovel-shaped feet a pinky-white. They will hang there for
months, until their bodies decay or get eaten away. Any survivors that are
left burrowing away beneath the riverbank may not have much of a new
year to enjoy. The mole-catcher will be back, tracking them down,
hanging them up, walking miles and miles in cold pursuit.

Professional mole-catchers have always been among the real characters
of the fens and, I must say, usually have a respect for wild-life that is

harmless. Their job takes them out into remote areas of the region where few other people get. They are "loners" and get to know as much about the land and its creatures as the farmer and wildfowler put together. They know where the kingfishers will build, where they might see an otter and, of course, where all the moles go underground and where to set their traps. One season's kill can amount to several hundred moles being strung up on fences throughout the fens. And it's not only on New Year's Day that they turn my stomach over.

I walk on towards a silence so full of the old year's death, towards a misty distance that shows no sign of spring, no glimmer of prosperity. Why have the bells stopped ringing? Where has the dark man gone? The only living thing along this bank this morning is the heron, the old, grey heron who stands like an undertaker at the edge of the river's grave.

I can understand why, at this time of the year, I am sometimes asked why I stay on speaking terms with this wet, bleak landscape. What can I see in it? What is there to write about? But a landscape is more than what can be seen just on the surface. It is more than the pattern of fields, hedges, rivers or hills that make up the visual appeal. Landscapes have qualities below the surface. Qualities that have to be felt and understood. Qualities that you cannot easily disown if they are part of you. Perhaps that is the only answer I can give.

> 'What is there? The fields stare back
> at the sky, asking whose fault is it
> that the earth looks empty. No cattle
> give life to the flat landscape, no hedges
> enclose the results of a man's labour.
> You can understand why the sea has withdrawn
> allowing the wind to inhabit this kingdom . . .'
>
> But speed-up the film that your eye is taking.
> Ten million roots thrust leaves up to the sun
> where the harvest is growing It's no-one's fault
> that the land looks empty. Things happen here
> in slow and subtle ways. There is a pact
> between the earth and sky as there is
> between a man and the seasons . . .
>
> And me?
> Why do I never leave for a land where stone-walls
> cast their nets over green hillsides?

I might perhaps, when these roots wither
and I can break out of the sky's cage
for some other freedom.

The question will be asked again. I may ask it of myself many times. I might even consider breaking out only to find that "some other freedom" is a new kind of prison.

Sometimes I think that winter is over sooner than we realize. The sap begins to rise in the darkest months, both in us and in nature. We only see the flowering. We seldom feel the tide turn. And on a day like this I look beyond the mist, I look deeper into this landscape's muddy crust. A million roots are already stirring deep in the soil, thrusting their leaves towards the sun that is yet to come. It is not always easy to believe, especially when the fields are still under snow or floods. This winter has been one of the wettest on record, and it's just as well that some of these washlands will not be needed for crops, for they are still under water. The expanse of water emphasizes the area of land. A five-barred gate stands in the middle of a flooded field like the skeleton of a stranded boat. The river-bank on the south side is no more than a length of wet rope dividing two stretches of water. The town is hidden away behind the damp curtain of air that draws itself over the land, intensifying the silence. And this is not the end of winter. There may be more snow to come, more floods, more fogs and frosts before those hiding seeds force their way into the light of spring. It is not easy to believe, but we have to believe. The land *will* know again the colour of green and the sound of larks; it will grow warm again and respond to the sun that is yet to come. I tell it to myself over and over again, not aloud, but inside, deep where all hopes thrust their leaves towards the spring.

A Beginning Again

What is there about midnight that makes it such a different hour from all the others of the day or night? Surely it is more than just the boundary between one day and another. More than the stile over which Time climbs. More than the division on a calendar. It is all these, of course, but it is also something else, something that makes the twelve strokes of midnight a tense and compelling hour never felt at mid-day.

I am sitting in my room alone, enjoying the silence that night brings;

listening to the silence, for it is almost audible. Perhaps it is not so much *silence* as *stillness*. Everywhere is very, very still. My neighbours are away and I can feel the emptiness of their house. The curtains of my room are drawn but I can feel the darkness of the garden outside and the darkness of the night.

The fire is burnt out and the grey ash from the last log is dead and still. I look at my watch. There are two minutes to go to twelve o'clock. I find it almost impossible to go to bed before midnight. As I've said before I feel as if I have wasted part of the day to think of sleeping before the early hours of the morning. "To kill time is to injure eternity," wrote Thoreau, and this last hour of the day, when I am absolutely alone, is not killing or wasting time but using it to absorb the stillness of the night, to collect all the wayward thoughts that have not been given much attention during the day.

I know it is a fallacy to believe that at such an hour I have the world all to myself while everyone else is asleep. I know there are thousands of other people awake, at work, or at clubs, nursing or watching, travelling or patrolling. But here, in this room, I am alone. The doors are locked. The world outside is quiet. The only sounds come from the watch on my wrist ticking those minutes away, and my pen scratching rhythmically on the page as I write.

I seldom write straight on to the typewriter. I love the feeling of the pen being an extension of my arm and hand. It is an extra finger through which the thoughts can flow. The pleasure of making signs on the page that become the words and sentences is, for me, an essential part of the creative process. The written word is still one of our most marvellous inventions—a few symbols drawn in various ways which allow us to communicate across both distance and time. To enjoy this sensation in the stillness of the day's last hour adds to the excitement of writing. A typewriter would violate all that this hour stands for. It would create noise where there should be silence. The joy of writing is also a personal discovery of the unknown and has to be achieved alone. I believe that I achieve it best when I think the rest of the world is asleep and I am the only person awake and at work.

Certainly tonight I am the only person awake in this house and, perhaps, the only person in the region who will be writing until two o'clock in the morning, persuading the words to sit still on the page. Anything beyond this neighbourhood now feels very distant. Even the sounds of a church clock chiming midnight sounds miles away, as if it is coming from some city under the sea.

There is a whisper of wind in the chimney and a flake of white ash stirs in the grate. There is the far-off sound of a train and the weak howl of a prowling cat. Then all is still again and I return with great expectancy to the silence of midnight, waiting for the tension to snap, waiting for the moment of creation to begin.

When this happens everything begins to come alive for me. The paintings on the wall appear to have more colour and more life. The books on my shelves are so real they nearly speak. The stillness gathers intensity. The blood flows more eagerly. The energy of every muscle concentrates and directs itself into these shapes and signs that are slowly conquering the awful blankness of the page; phrases and sentences that will, with luck, still be there when I wake up in the morning.

Is it because I was born at two minutes to midnight that I always come alive so, I wonder? Whatever it is the magic hour does a Cinderella-in-reverse and I shed the ordinary chores of the day to enjoy an hour or two in writing, reading, listening, or just being awake when I imagine the world is asleep. Does it matter if it's all make-believe? If nothing else happens I have had the silence.

If I am unwise to expect some sort of victory over the blank page every night there is at least one night of the year when I do feel that the last few moments are significant. Then, in that birthday hour, I know I am one who has been long acquainted with the night. Then, as the clock's hands hesitate towards midnight, I want ideas and sensations to come more willingly to the mind's magnet. Then I want the hour to draw the mind back as far as it can to the beginning. . . .

Only the movement of birds
gives life to winter.
Sky has no heart-beat,
sunrise no wonder.

Only silence is heard.
Ice hardens grasses.
Days are so earth-bare
light never passes.

Child of earth's iron
caught in your birth room,
remember that midnight
of star-talk and fortune.

Remember the waiting
and grief that was given.
Coax words into fire
or pray to be barren.

Now with earth's snowfall
and hunger in houses,
three months of frost
and the father's cheeks hollow;

take in your small hands
the gifts of your season,
sing for a summer
though flowers are frozen.

Child of earth's iron,
dead grass and furrow,
dance for your birth-night
or shrivel in sorrow.

The journey there and the journey back pass quickly. Thankfully fire always burns through the sorrow and summer always dances beneath the wet grass. The years feel no more than a sequence of heart-beats. When I wake in the morning it will be a new month and then a new season. In a few weeks' time we shall all move back into an orbit of warmth and light. Then I shall sit by this window and the sun will jump gently into my lap like a friendly cat wanting somewhere to sleep for the day. Then the days will be long with far-away skies and the trees will be full of unfolding buds and hatching eggs. Then a new journey will begin, taking familiar routes over a country travelled before, but this time it will be different.

It will be different because you can never look twice at this earth with the same eyes. Everything will be older, even the land and the sun's light. Even the distance between the water and stars.

PART FOUR

SPRING LIGHT AND FULL CIRCLE

"Each new year is a surprise to us. We find that we had virtually forgotten the note of each bird and when we hear it again it is remembered like a dream, reminding us of a previous state of existence."

Thoreau: March 18th 1858

Freedom

I WOULD ALWAYS come back to this land, as I said at the beginning, for the low light of evening and the bright day's awakening. Light has been a recurring theme in this journal and being made aware of it again on this spring morning I suppose it is the one quality of the fen country that is most difficult to convey in words. One can talk about distance in terms of miles. It is possible to describe the flat land of rivers and farms. One can talk about the character of the people and give some idea of the great skies. But how can I write of the light in the fens so that a stranger might know what I mean?

It is an elusive quality that I am after. It is true to say that some days there is a dazzling spread of light over the whole land that makes everything shine. It is true to say that some days there is a very soft lustre in the air that gives every house and field a quiet beauty far removed from winter's bleakness. It is a light that gives clarity and sharpness. It is also a light that subdues and blurs. But it is always there, even on wet days, in each season of the year, and always it influences one's view of the landscape itself.

I was talking to my friend and illustrator, John Hutton, who is an artist and who has, I know, been faced with the same problem of catching this quality of light in his paintings. 'In a way,' he said, 'you are trying to paint something that isn't there and yet exists everywhere. It's like trying to paint *sound*. You can't give a colour to the light itself but because the light intensifies the colour of everything else you just know you have to do something about it.'

'I suppose it's like trying to paint the space we were talking about the other day?'

'Exactly . . . When you're painting on to a flat surface you can only succeed in painting a fen landscape if, somehow, you can paint the space that you know exists between the horizon and the sky. And on a day like this you have to aim for that brilliance that exists between the object and the sun. You find that you are trying to take something out of the picture all the time to make way for the light.'

'But you succeed from time to time, don't you? I mean, you get the feeling of translucence shining through so that we are seeing more than is actually on the canvas?'

'I'd like to think I get fairly near at times. As you know, I have spent years painting light through mist, light on snow, light on farm-buildings, light on brickyard chimneys and the light at each end of the day. But there's always something that gets away, always something that you know you've missed. And let's face it, we are after the impossible.'

So when I fail in my efforts to describe the quality of this light I know the problem is shared and that it is extremely difficult to even suggest the effect that the light has on this land. It is not just the quality of light one gets in the sky. It is what happens to familiar things around you that are suddenly transformed by that light. Often when I am out walking or driving I have to stop because I have noticed a wall or a tree that I have never really looked at before. The light may have settled on a square of bricks or the red roof tiles of a barn, or it may have crept through the undergrowth and transferred itself to the green bark of a tree, and immediately there is something very beautiful being made out of the ordinary and familiar. Everything gives back this light, so the impact is multiplied. Every clod of a newly-ploughed field, every blade of grass, every drop of water in the rivers and dykes, every wing of the lark, every gate and tree, shines with this light. And on a day like this the earth sparkles.

I do not have to explain now how the seasons of the year influence my work and give direction to my thoughts. Again I have come full circle and it is spring. Although the years differ and the seasons vary from year to year I think I would be prepared to say that spring is, in many ways, the same in any year. The temperature may change. The first flowers may be late in arriving, the cold winds reluctant to leave. But spring is spring. It is always the new beginning. The start of another journey. The birth of new expectations however old or cynical we may become. The light of spring lifts a year's work off our shoulders and the next year feels, in its present infancy, already more bearable.

By the time that summer is here the year is well established and we know of the half that is gone and half-know of what is to be. Autumn confirms our fears or successes, tells us with some evidence whether we are having a good year or bad. And winter gives us time in which to reflect on the seasons that have gone, allowing us time to cogitate on our mistakes or to sit back for a little while to enjoy the results of our labours. It is as if nature forces the spirit to hibernate during the grey days so that it can experience the pleasure of waking again a month or so later to respond more eagerly to a sky and earth that are golden.

Spring, on the other hand, is too young to know disappointment and too new to feel jaded. It is the one season of the year we can trust. We join with the flowers and birds' eggs in being part of a rebirth. We get into step with the rest of the earth, pushing the roots down deeper into our soil, spreading our leaves more and more to catch the sun. It is the most positive time of our year. We become part of the great thaw and get carried along on the melting snow. Everything about spring is filled with this purposefulness. The sounds, colours, smells and tastes are all bright, joyful things. Take, for instance, the spring flowers and consider their colours. Those "fair maids of February" the snowdrops, give us a pure colour to start with, and soon the crocus, daffodil and primrose gild the dark earth with yellow and gold. It is not an accident that the predominant colours of spring are yellow and bright green, for these are the colours of triumph. In addition to the daffodils and forsythia in the garden the cowslip, celandine and buttercup of the wayside come like trumpeters to announce earth's pageantry. They are all part of the season's heraldry. Just as blue is the colour of "sapphires, deep water and loyalty", just as red is the colour of "rubies, revelry, courage and magic", just as purple is the colour of "amethysts, royalty and death", so green is the colour of "emeralds, hope, youth and spring" and gold is the colour of "reliability and triumph". Could it be otherwise?

Of all the spring flowers none gives me a greater feeling of wonder and excitement than the primrose. I know it is not predominant among the other shapes and shades of spring but to find the first primrose of the year is always one of the year's joys. To see that first modest flower tucked away in a copse of winter-parched bramble takes my breath away. That it should have survived and blossomed again is as good as any miracle.

I try not to pick the very first flower I see. It is too precious, too lovely. I want to leave it in that half-hidden position for someone else to find, to feel perhaps the same pleasure. But I shall look for others, even though they are hard to find in our part of the country.

Legend says that the first primrose one sees in spring is a magic flower and the key to happiness. Any door you wish to be opened to you will open if touched with the first primrose of the year. Persephone, returning from her captivity in the underworld, greeted her mother with so many tears of gratitude that suddenly a multitude of primroses blossomed at her feet. Each spring the primrose celebrates her freedom and, I think, our freedom too. It is a flower full of meaning and symbolism, which may explain our own desire to be the first person to find one each year. They are the flowers which, Shakespeare said, "die unmarried ere they can behold bright Phoebus in his strength".

But as I was saying, before getting sidetracked into the memory of

K

legends, the fen country is not good primrose country. Not only are we virtually without woods or spinneys but the flower does not care for our soil either. To look for primroses we have to go on to the higher ground on the western boundary of the fens where there are still a few haunts left in which they can survive, where no major road works have, as yet, sent in the bulldozers to rip out their ancient roots from the land. How long this will be so I don't know. Not long, I imagine. Many woods have been lost around the Peterborough area in the last few years as the expansion plans move more and more into the surrounding villages and countryside. Twenty years ago we could walk quite easily to quiet corners and undisturbed woods where wildflowers grew in abundance. Not now. Those woods are only found now on out-of-date maps. The footpaths are somewhere beneath the new dual carriageways. The flowers gone. Now we have to drive several miles to find an undiscovered dykeside or copse where the primrose plant struggles for survival against more than the developer.

I prefer to find the flower in the woods rather than in the dykes. There's something very primitive about trampling through a spring wood that smells of wild garlic, with the sound of twigs snapping under your feet and a frightened pheasant jumping up in front of you. To be back again among the thorny undergrowth and the soft earth, to be surrounded by trees and aware of the blue sky high above their silent branches is still a very satisfying experience.

But more and more these secret places are being discovered and the plants of wildflowers are uprooted for surburban rockeries. The woods are littered with old cans, bicycles, tyres, mattresses, all the rubbish that people don't want and assume that nature does. Why doesn't it occur to them that man who has created so much waste for his own world should also accept the responsibility of getting rid of it in his world? There are, after all, corporation tips and many other facilities for disposing of unwanted armchairs and bed-springs without dumping them in the countryside along with all the broken bottles, newspapers and plastic containers that spoil most beauty spots. It's as much an act of vandalism to dump rubbish in the countryside as it is to deface public buildings or to rip out the seats of railway compartments. It's the same mentality. The disease is the same. Nothing infuriates a farmer more than to see the headlands of a newly ploughed or sown field littered next morning with a car-load of junk that someone has thrown out in the night for him to clear up. Nothing is more annoying than to find a spring spinney full of someone's discarded sitting-room or garage.

Last year we noticed that one of our favourite places had been discovered by the litter-dumpers and this year the stone walls are broken
down, the undergrowth torn apart, the birds have gone and the flowers
huddle in some remote corner like little frightened animals. So this year
we pick the first primroses we find with something like urgency, as if to
rescue them from the next set of car wheels and bed-springs.

> You pick them—
> the few flowers that have survived
> the coarse tracks of machines
> and the vanishing act of trees.
>
> I know once
> there were enough blossoms for us both
> to stroll into these woods and begin
> picking, without any searching.
>
> The pale heads
> met us at the wood's boundary
> like sheep gathered by a stone wall,
> or children out in their school playground.
>
> But not now.
> What copse is left for the wild primrose
> is a poor wilderness on the edge
> of an airfield, abundant with noise.
>
> Only in this
> bare hollow, littered with old cans,
> have we found any survivors
> of our earlier springs.
>
> Small-petalled,
> short-stemmed, timid as field-mice,
> they stare at us, unsure and vulnerable.
> You pick them, hold them, take them home.

I can't help remembering two springs ago, when we were in Cornwall,
how we gasped in audible envy when we saw the quiet lanes there piled
up with flowers as deep as a yellow snowdrift. Now, I thought, if we
could have such generous springs. . . . But then I changed my mind. The
search for the few survivors made our springs all the more real, all the

more significant and meaningful. And, in our part of the country, I suppose we must see the primrose as some kind of bonus anyway. We have the country's biggest fields coming to life, the acres of daffodils coming into bloom, the cereal crops growing. Go out on any spring day and you will see activity scattered all over the fens. The farm gates have been opened. The fields have been unwrapped. The men are back on the land. The earth is awake. It's so difficult to know where to be on a day like this when so many favourite horizons call.

I return again to Crowland and then to the banks of the River Welland where the water is flowing swiftly towards Spalding. Along Deeping High Bank the fields drop away quite dramatically below the level of the water, and although the road itself is hardly above sea-level there is the feeling of being on the edge of a cliff—so low are the fields of Deeping St Nicholas Fen and the land that spreads away into the distance for twenty miles.

The sky is a very soft blue with the net-like clouds allowing the light to shimmer. The light today is almost touchable, it is so vivid, so much a part of the day. I feel that all I want to do is to sit here staring into the distance for as long as possible. The longer I look the more amazed I become at the land's vastness, at its ability to excite and inspire, to subdue and overawe. I feel that the longer I stay the stronger my eyes become so that what was unseen ten minutes ago is now within my vision. The sky has the subtle changing nuances of a water-colour slowly drying on paper, but beyond those shades is the great secret we cannot capture on paper or canvas, in paint or words.

I take the road that dips down into the fen and drive slowly towards the bulb fields of Lincolnshire. Daffodils, like tulips, are a major crop in these northern fens and the fields around Spalding, Holbeach, Whaplode and Pinchbeck are already yellow with a million flowers waiting to be picked or de-headed. Often the flowers are incidental.

Bulb-growing has been one of the big successes on this silt land of Lincolnshire, and in seventy-five years the acreage has grown from three hundred to over ten thousand acres a year, producing bulbs of top quality and variety. When the crops are in bloom this part of the fen country is, for a brief period, put on the tourists' maps, and coaches from distant parts of England make their way between multi-coloured fields, culminating in the enormous gathering on the Saturday chosen for the Spalding Tulip Festival.

That climax is still to come. The roads are still empty and the fields have their glory all to themselves. Under today's light these spaces have an even greater magnitude. They appear to go on for a hundred miles, and yet only a few miles away the sea says "stop" and in the opposite direction the uplands close their gates to the eyes' adventure. What creates this illusion of extraordinary distance? Again it must be the light acting as a magnifying-glass, enlarging the fields so that we see them as double their size, extending the normal peripheries beyond twice their limits.

I drive again along the western boundary of the fens, through the cluster of villages known as "The Deepings"—Market Deeping, Deeping St James and West Deeping—sharing the banks of the River Welland and a collection of warm stone houses that look as lovely as the Cotswolds after the brick buildings of Cambridgeshire.

These villages too, have a history that goes back before the Romans and early Britons, before even the fens themselves were formed. Skeletons of prehistoric animals have been preserved in the clay and gravel. Bones of mammoths, boars, buffalo, bears and deer that were hunted long before we settled for duck-shooting and fishing, have been ploughed up within recent years. The discovery of Roman pottery and coins has been commonplace by comparison with other areas and has given a clear picture of the importance of Market Deeping two thousand years ago.

At Market Deeping I am reminded again of St Guthlac of Crowland, who passed through these villages on his way from Ripon to establish his own hermitage and abbey in the fens. The parish church is dedicated to him and, at one time, the town was known as Deeping St Guthlac. There are also two interesting phrases printed on the church tower which are not seen by everyone but are worth mentioning. Leaving the town in the morning as you travel northwards you read "The Day is Thine". Returning in the evening you are welcomed back by the words "The Night Cometh". The texts are, of course, only appropriate if you travel in these directions and it is reasonable to assume that when they were written most of the Deeping people would have gone north to the neighbouring market town of Bourne rather than south to Peterborough. But today, with new housing estates on the north side of the church, commuters into the city must read into the words what they can. I can imagine for many of them with boring jobs and lives of great pressure that "The Night Cometh" offers a ray of hope as they set out and, in the evening when they return, "The Day is Thine" has a touch of irony.

For me the words say what they were meant to say, as I take the road for Baston, Thurlby and Bourne. The north calls me again and I find it a considerable temptation to go up into the Lincolnshire Wolds and Tennyson's country. There are some interesting villages there with good panoramas over the lowlands to the coast and attractive woodland rides over the hills. But the only diversion I make is to pull off the main road for a while to watch a man ploughing. He has no doubts about his day's journey, no wild yearnings to be somewhere else. He will not have to take notice of road-signs or stop at traffic-lights. For today and tomorrow and for the whole of his year his world will be the fields he has worked for many seasons. He knows every movement of the earth. He knows every change in the wind's direction and what the clouds mean. He has time to feel and to know. When I leave him to his work in search of my own I am partly jealous, partly grateful.

He had it all to himself,
ploughing alone in a field
the size of a continent.

There was the day's new warmth,
the unexpected light
released from a cold sky.

Even the gulls did not find him
and the larks ventured too high
to be part of his earth.

He owned that remarkable space
not to be found in cities
or where the hills brood.

He went out and came back
all day on the long wake
of his own sailing,

a monotonous journey
with only sleep and a ploughed field
for his destination.

There will be other days
when the rain will try out its nails
on his parched face,

when the undisciplined wind
will blunt every wave
of his black sea,

> but these he will patiently bear
> rather than turn into our world
> where there are no seasons.

Fortunately, I do not have to turn back to the city either and can enjoy the freedom of the day even though I have two calls to make in Bourne. Between Spalding and Bourne there are several isolated roads and waterways to explore, roads that might not be attempted in winter but can hardly be resisted on a high spring day. The slight breeze blowing in from the Wash is as pure and sweet as mountain air. The water in the streams and drains is almost as blue as the sky.

After lunch I visit one of the schools in Bourne and then call to see some friends who live nearby. When I return home in the evening it is still quite warm and light and I am in no hurry to shorten the day by shutting myself indoors sooner than I need. At Northborough I turn off the main road again into the old part of the village and stop for a moment at the grey church and churchyard where John Clare's widow is buried, a woman who had to bear so much of the poet's unhappy time in Northborough and who tried unsuccessfully to keep him from being taken away to the Northampton General Lunatic Asylum, where he was to remain for the next twenty-three years.

I always find it difficult to pass the Northborough cottage without feeling its sadness and tragedy. Clare's birthplace at Helpston knew none of those final shadows and still belongs in his work to the happier years of his life. The renovated cottage there, is, for that reason, more attractive, even though Clare himself never knew such comfort. But the Northborough cottage is haunted by the fears and the despair, by the dust and ashes of his early fame. Clare could not accept Northborough and could not find contentment there, even though he walked the eighty-four miles home to it from Dr Allan's private asylum at High Beech in Epping Forest. "I seem," Clare wrote,

> Alone and in a stranger scene
> Far from spots my heart esteems . . .
>
> Strange scenes mere shadows are to me
> Vague unpersonifying things . . .
>
> Here every tree is stranger to me,
> All foreign things where'er I go . . .

Northborough and the surrounding fens had taken Clare away from his own Eden, from his own natural source of creation. He was totally unable to reconcile himself with his new home. Not only had he lost the brief fame that his early poetry had brought, he had also lost Helpston and the scenes of his childhood. By comparison the world of nature now looked very ordinary, the hedges were "a deader green", the sun was "a homeless ranger" that pursued "a naked weary way / Unnoticed like a very stranger." Even the clouds and water lost their magic:

> The stream it is a naked stream
> Where we on Sundays used to ramble,
> The sky hangs o'er a broken dream,
> The brambles dwindled to a bramble . . .

Clare did not transplant easily. His roots were still in the open pasture fields and woodlands of Northamptonshire. Having lost the security of the familiar, having been expelled from his innocent world, he could only see his life as "a shipwreck". When he returned home to Northborough from Epping Forest he was allowed to stay in his cottage there for just a further four months. In December 1841 he was removed to the General Lunatic Asylum at Northampton, where he stayed until he died in 1864. His widow, Martha Clare, continued to live in this village with more than one sorrow. In 1843 her son Frederick died and a year later she lost her daughter Anna. In 1852 the youngest child, Charles (who showed considerable promise and was greatly loved by his father), also died and ten years later she lost Sophia. Within twelve months she was to hear from friends at Helpston that her husband's body had been brought home from Northampton to his native village for burial. She had not seen him since he was taken away twenty-three years earlier. They had been twenty-three very hard years for her as well as for her husband.

No, it is not easy to pass the cottage this evening, or at any other time, without remembering those days and the words that grew out of their agony. Was it a coincidence that those years of depression and low spirit in the poet's life came with his brief stay in the flat lowlands of Lincolnshire? Did he and the landscape become one? Did he draw from that enforced landscape the imagery that he needed to explore and express his new feelings? Was the dreary scene a fitting background to his melancholy, or did the landscape itself finally destroy him because he could not get his troubled spirit to take root in alien soil? Can a landscape destroy a writer as much as it can make one?

All night I've coveted your painting of cool light,
envying the clear economy of line with which
you've fixed in shapes all that escapes my syllables.

There hung our common themes – bright water, space, and sky
reaching towards infinity . . .

It is significant, I think, that during the twenty-three years of exile Clare returned again and again in his imagination to the scenes of his youth—to Helpston rather than to Northborough. It was fortunate for the ageing man that his early years had given him so much and that his memory had preserved it for him. He could write of a Helpston spring fifty years later and still make it seem as fresh as this year's spring. There has not been a greater landscape poet. The cottage at Northborough, with all its good intentions, stands in the evening light like a question-mark.

The road continues along an ancient track, near a Roman dyke, and eventually joins the road to Peakirk where there is now a popular Wildfowl Trust with a collection of rare and rich-plumaged ducks and geese.

Tucked away in the trees is a hermitage with a history that goes back to the eighth century and owes its foundation to one of St Guthlac's family. This is believed to have been Guthlac's sister, Pega, to whom the parish church is dedicated.

I pass the church, the village green and the long narrow pub called The Ruddy Duck, and half decide to go to Glinton. The tall slender spire of its church cuts like a pair of scissors into the sky. The western horizon is still quite light but eastwards I can see the darkness quickly rising, so that for a few moments I look up and see two different skies meeting above my head. This hesitation persuades me to leave Glinton for another day, and take instead the less-travelled road into Werrington, a village that has been swallowed whole by the growth of Peterborough, and yet has managed somehow to retain its identity as a village with thatched cottages, church, and green.

For a moment I think I see the house-martins back, but when I look again at the little black shapes flitting between the trees I realize that they are bats. The hour is just right for them. The sky is now a deep bilberry colour, the trees are dark navy. Nine o'clock chimes from the bell-tower and the street is so quiet it could be midnight.

Reflections

I don't think I have ever seen the Nene more still than it is this morning. When I came to it an hour ago it was only vaguely there beneath the mist. But then the mist weighed anchor and an armada of sailing ships moved slowly downstream, leaving the surface of the water motionless, deserted in its own silence, without the faintest ripple.

It is now a shining stillness on which every reflection is a perfectly inverted replica of the original: pylons, fences, two cows by the water's edge, the sluice gates and the sky, are all mirrored in such a faultless image that it would not matter much if the world suddenly turned over. The scene would be the same.

The water is not grey or blue, not brown or green, but has a silvery sheen on the pink of the sky that goes down to the river-bed. If you could see all the fish down there today they would be technicoloured, and the mud would look not unlike strawberry mousse.

A lapwing flies from one bank to the other and I do not even look up but watch its journey in the water. It lands on the grass opposite and jerks its head guiltily as if it has just done something wrong.

The sun grows warmer now as it rises over the town and soon all the signs of the mist have disappeared and the pink of the water changes to gold. A lark is singing just a few feet away from me. He is joined by another and soon, all round me, is a shower of lark song, each note, each drop is 22-carat gold chiming all the way down to this water's edge.

It has been worth coming out this early in the morning even though my stay must be brief. It is a day that could keep me out of doors until dark, but it is also a day on which I have let too many jobs fall, and so I must return to my desk.

As I get back to the car four swans fly over the sluice and along the straight stretch of the river that goes towards Peterborough, their white and graceful formation reflected in the water; they fly low and straight, vain enough, perhaps, to watch themselves in the mirror below.

I start the car and follow them. We journey almost parallel for nearly two miles at a steady twenty-five miles an hour. Then, realizing perhaps that they are being watched, they veer off over the fields, their long necks pointing towards the sun, their big wings rhythmically beating the air.

At the end of the river-bank I look back and the shining expanse of water is very difficult to leave. But I tell myself that already there are ripples on its surface and soon the stillness will be spoilt. Stillness doesn't last for long. We have to capture and preserve its magic in whatever way we can. At the moment it is printed clearly on my mind and, I hope, in the few words that I wrote down when I was afraid to turn the notebook's page ten minutes ago. How much of it can I preserve for the hours that are left?

The day has been bright and blue all morning and afternoon. I have looked out like a prisoner longing to escape, longing for his eight-hour sentence to end, longing for the light to stay so that I can get out again into the countryside, to sit by the river or to walk over a field.

Everything has had some element of beauty in it today. The red roof-tops of my neighbours' houses and the walls have all been glazed with light. A nearby telegraph pole has looked so alive it could have sprouted leaves. The young leaves on the trees dazzled as they opened. The garden woke up and made music.

"There are from time to time," wrote Thoreau, "mornings, both in summer and winter, when especially the world seems to begin anew, beyond which the memory need not go. . . ." This morning was that kind of morning and the whole day has been a continuance of its blessing, a day when we are re-united with some forgotten dream, reminding us of a "previous state of existence".

If tomorrow is like today I know I shall have to go out into the solitude and silence of the countryside where life is simple, and where the warmth and light of the sun will do more in one hour than eight hours' sleep could ever achieve.

It's a familiar conflict. When I'm working at my desk I feel I ought to be out in some part of that country from which all the ideas come and which I might lose by not being there. And when I'm out among the fields and under the victorious sky from which so much inspiration comes I feel that I ought to be at my desk working, doing something about the ideas. Really one wants to be in two places at once.

I suppose this is one of the advantages of having seasons: in winter it is easier to stay at home when the days are short and cold, but in spring, with the land coming to life and the days lengthening then the spirit longs to be part of that rebirth. So then I compromise. I use the excitement of the morning to keep me going for several hours and then I escape once more into the open air as evening comes. . . .

The light on the fields is again very dramatic. Every stalk, twig or blade of grass, every plant or clod of earth reflects the setting sun. Once again the low light flows gently over the land until it glimmers like a calm sea. The reeds in the dykes are alight, their feathers golden. The water dazzles as bright as mercury. And slowly the colours deepen from gold into bronze until the earth is like burnished metal. Darkness follows.

Unfoldings

The days' excitements are piling up, layer on layer. I find myself driving quickly to favourite places, not knowing where to settle. I stop the car and run along a river-bank. I pick up a handful of earth. I fill my lungs with the air. I sit for a few moments on a five-barred gate and then I'm off again to drive on quiet roads where rabbits still run and where the wild-flowers are beginning to grow again. In one field I see a woman plough-ing, her strong arms keeping a straight furrow. At a nearby house another woman is hanging out her clothes to dry. It's a good day for a wash-day. The white of the sheets is quite brilliant against a background of black earth and blue sky. Washing on the line is still a healthy sight in the fens. The wind fills the sheets until they strain to be free and join the clouds. It's what the local women call "good blowing country" and clothes that have not been dried out-doors on the line never smell the same, they say. The woman pegging out her washing looks over to the woman who is ploughing and sees the wake of white gulls blowing like a line of handker-chiefs. The woman ploughing glances occasionally at the garden of washing and sees the wind in the sails of the ship she is sailing.

I make my way back towards Thorney and then on to Whittlesey, crossing the Nene again and then Morton's Leam. I go into the town, pass the Buttercross and market square and drive out into the black fens beyond Benwick and Chatteris. There is something happening everywhere. The buildings look different. Houses shine. People move with more purpose. The land vibrates. The floods of winter are already being distanced by the excitement of spring, by the joy at being out again with so much freedom. I find myself almost going round in circles. Each horizon beckons.

It's a day for a pub lunch and I call at a local where I know a few old men with nothing better to do than talk an hour or two away will be re-living a score of springs. Memories preserve not only events but also phrases, sayings or variations of proverbs that might otherwise get lost, such as:

A rotten stick in a hedge always cracks first.

or

It's like trying to find a smile in church.

I sit talking with two men who meet every Tuesday in this bar. The younger-looking one assures me, with ill-disguised pride, that he is eighty-eight, while the older-looking one reluctantly admits that he is only seventy-six.

'I know,' he said, with a boredom that suggests he has explained it many times before, 'you think we got that mixed-up, don't you? Well, we ain't, and the reason why this old davil looks younger'n me is because he's never 'ad to work as 'ard as what I 'ev.'

'Well, that's nothin' but a lot o' lies, that ain't,' said the other. 'I was a-workin' afore yew were ever born, that I wer, and that's as true as I sit here and yew know it. . . .'

'Maybe yew was, but that don't mean to say that yew've worked 'arder 'an what I 'ev. Yew spent arf your time in the army.'

The eighty-eight-year-old looked at me with a broad smile that confirmed they had been through all this argument before, week after week. And the ageing seventy-six grouser wasn't going to let him off the hook yet.

'How many winters have yew spent in the fens, yew tell me that? Yew were away for more 'an ten years, weren't yew, so that makes no more than seventy-eight and arf of them yew've spent under cover. . . . Ain't that right?'

I asked him if he'd never thought of an indoor job.

'Me? I've worked out-doors all my life . . . I left school when I was thirteen and I've worked on the land ever since, winter and summer. . . . It's the winters what age a man. I've worked for days wet through to the skin, in wind and frost, and when I've bin hungry. . . . No wonder I'm crippled with rheumatism. It's all right for 'im, he's allus 'ad someone to cook for 'im and look after 'im. I've lived on my own this last eight year and that's been a long time.'

The older man smiled and shook his head. 'That's one thing, bor, old Job will never be dead while you're alive, that 'e won't. Yew're allus moaning about somethin'. That's a wonder yew ain't been dead this long time.'

I tried to lift the gloom by asking them whether they thought we were going to have a good summer.

'Of course we are,' said the cheerful one, looking fit enough for at least another decade. 'I think we're in for a very good summer.'

'I doubt it myself,' said Jo, 'that's been a wet winter and yew can never forget how much ache there's been on the land even when the crops start to grow. It's been too wet for the seed and we don't get summers like we used to get years ago. The fields know, and I know. I've never 'ad an indoor job all my life, which is more than yew can say about some people. . . .'

It was a thought I pursued into a new poem:

>They are still there
>under the green filter of spring wheat.
>Summer will not hide them
>nor any crops that may be planted out.
>The lark knows it,
>so too does the man whose creaking joints
>remember the winters
>of ice-rain and wind-chap. A shadow haunts
>each harvest reaped
>and when long sunlight warms the land
>split fingers will still ache
>with frost and mud long buried in the mind.
>
>So much is there
>beneath the wealth of flower and ripe grain.
>Hunger and dole-queues gnaw
>at the deep roots of memory in those men
>whose fathers knew
>the unpaid idleness such winters gave.
>Some things have changed, but not
>the fields that can absorb both hate and love.
>Soot-black as night
>they are but camouflaged for spring.
>Unlike the ransomed lark
>these earthbound men have little time for song.

Having aired all his grievances the local Job began to talk quite seriously about his life in the fens and the fens themselves. He had a real love-hate relationship with the land and his short, staccato sentences became a soliloquy as we sat listening. . . .

'What a lot of people don't realize is that we made it, we made this land what it is. We have made the fields and the roads. We even made the rivers. . . . I get tired of that lot from the city who come to live out 'ere on the new estates and say they're going to put this place on the map. . . . *We* put it on the map three hundred years ago—my father's father's people did that, generation after generation. No, I don't like change. I don't like to see us losing the land as quickly as we are. . . . Yew could say I'm suspicious, even resentful. I like to see faces I know, hear voices I can recognize. It's like being in a foreign country at times, especially 'ere in the pub. This car-park's full at the week-ends. Yew get all sorts. Oh, they leave us alone, granted. The visitors use the lounge bar and get all the service. We stay in 'ere and take no notice if they come in to gawk at us. Perhaps yew're right, they do keep the place going. I can remember when this place used to be full, every night with just village people. We 'ad scores of pubs 'ere at one time. . . . Characters? Good lork-a-day, bor, there were some characters all right. People knew 'ow to be different then. They didn't copy one another's clothes in them days like they do today. You wore what you could get 'old of and then wore them out, patches an' all. . . . Sing-songs? Ah, we used to have a good old sing 'ere once upon a time, especially on Saturday nights. We used to have a chap from the Salvation Army come in to sell his papers and he'd sing "The Old Rugged Cross" for us over and over again and we all used to join in the chorus—I bet I could remember the words now. But 'e don't come any more. It's like I say, things 'ev changed a lot. . . .

'Well, we allus moan more as we get older, don't we? . . . We like to talk about the good old days, which weren't very good at all, but they stay in your mind because yew were young and knew how to enjoy yourself. We used to think that if we got drunk twice a week that we were 'aving a good time, but that's not very sensible when yew look back. . . . No, we didn't go out of town much. There was no need. I was thirty before I went over to Peterborough and I've never bin to London. Why not? I don't think there's anything there I particularly want to see now, what with bombs and robberies—you're safer staying at home. No, and I've never 'ed an holiday in my life . . . a bit of rabbit-shooting and fishing, perhaps, but never a holiday like some people 'ev, going away from home and that.'

And then he smiled. 'I'm on holiday now. . . . It's nice coming in here to talk about the old times. . . . I shall most likely die in here, which won'd be a bad way to go. And yew can take my word for it, we have the last laugh in the end. . . . Of course I mean it. . . . And I shall come back to haunt yew. When yew've bin 'ere as long as we 'ev yew don't let go that easy. . . .'

We? But who are we, I wondered, even if we have been here for generations? It is quite true that this land has been made the kind of land it is by the men who have worked it, saved it, protected it and farmed it for hundreds of years. But who were those men? Who lived here a thousand years ago? How many of those families have survived in the descendants who may still be here? Who were these men's ancestors? How many of the Normans stayed, or the Danes? And what about the Dutch who came to help Vermuyden? Or the Scottish prisoners-of-war who were brought down from Dunbar to increase his labour force? Or the French Huguenots? Who are we?

What is it that cries out of the root of our soul for an identity, a home-coming? Where do we belong? From where have we come? Do the centuries cancel out these beginnings? I feel my own soul so deeply imbedded in this soil that I believe the belonging is of some great age. But does it matter?

I think the answer is yes. Only one thing is missing out of this great past. Where is the music, the forgotten song heard in a forgotten cradle, the tune on a coarse fiddle or the chanted ballad? There must have been music once, for there is the rhythm's heritage in the blood and this daily search through the dark ancestry of words. But where now is the drum-beat or the lament sung round a wild, smoking fire? Where is the sad voice of that faraway woman, or the primitive dance that the long years have paralysed?

It is something I cannot find. The only music I hear is in the wind or played on the long gut of the telegraph wires. There are echoes in the air, but from where? To lose the continuity of song is to lose the colour of one's blood. Bartok knew this and it intensified his search. I search the mist and the fields, the homes and waters of this landscape. But the music remains elusive and faraway.

The more I search the more I praise. The more I praise the more aware I am of the conflict between what I feel and what I hear from other men, like the ones I have been talking to today. The hardship, suffering and misery that these fields have known are in conflict with my own accept-ance and need of them. The more I probe into their history the more I am haunted by their victims and the memories of men who have worked this land for their bread:

> Men have died there
> though they have taken their bodies home
>   for the ceremonial dying.
> They have handed over their keys
>   to the cold winds
> and closed their gates on the brooding waters.

Their song ended
though no-one heard from their crushed hearts
   the ancestral singing.
They have left their blood in the soil
   and their white bones
no longer bend to the land's seasons.

Only they know
how many secrets the furrows keep
   of their casual passing.
Though their bodies are washed in grief's tears
   they remain part
of the fields and shadow our boundaries.

New Roads on old Land

Today I went beyond Twentypence Road at Wilburton and on to
Stretham and Upware. It was a day that tempted me to go as far as Wicken
Fen to enjoy again the spring's sweet smells that rise from the piece of
original fen with its lodes, reeds, peat-paths, wildflowers, blossoms and
ponds. But the reason for extending my journey in the first place was to
go, eventually, to Swaffham Prior where I wanted to see the grave of the
Scottish poet, Edwin Muir. So when I reached the sign-post to Upware
I left the main road and drove down that narrow path into some of the
blackest fenland you can find anywhere in the country.

Between Upware, Reach and Swaffham Bulbeck is Adventurers' Fen
and Adventurers' Ground; land named after the Gentlemen Adventurers
who, in the seventeenth century, provided the capital for the vast drainage
operations that Cornelius Vermuyden still had to complete. The work was
not a success and many attempts were made to reclaim this area of land
during the next two hundred years.

Draining the fens has changed the features of this landscape many times
and the most successful work has been achieved by the engineers of the
late nineteenth and twentieth centuries. Even so, some fenland refused to
surrender without a long struggle, and this Adventurers' land between
Upware and Swaffham was completely waterlogged until 1940, when
the food shortage of the Second World War made it necessary to make
yet another attempt at draining Swaffham Fen to try to gain more land
for agricultural purposes. It was an effort not without its frustrations and

only the determination of a few individuals turned what could have been another failure into a success. Now there is this narrow road from Upware to Reach, to Burwell and the Swaffhams. It is a single-track road with passing-places and travels over the extremely black land that I have already mentioned. The soil at Holme Fen is black. Soot is black. But I am sure that the soil between Upware and Swaffham Prior is blacker still; a deep, rich, bright, dramatic black that makes even a fenman stop to admire its colour again.

Before taking the turn to Swaffham Prior there is a turning to the small village of Reach, a place that once knew much busier times when, in the fourteenth century, it was quite a prosperous inland port, owing its existence originally to an old Roman canal. The Romans had several settlements along this south-eastern boundary of the fens and they had cut canals from the main waterways to serve their communities. The canal which became known as Reach Lode knew important trade two thousand years ago, and fourteen hundred years later was still carrying cargoes of wheat, barley, timber, stone, sheep, horses and even wine. But by the nineteenth century its trade had declined and a new competitor had arrived to serve East Anglia—the railway. Now the village of Reach is a quiet, almost forgotten island in the fens where gulls follow the wake of the plough and the goods arrive in a grocer's-van.

From Reach it is only a mile or two to Swaffham Prior, a village on higher ground, with attractive houses, cottage gardens and tall trees round the manor.

The first unusual thing that you notice about it is that the churchyard has not one, but two churches. One is dedicated to St Mary and the other to Saints Cyria and Jullita. It is not quite certain why Swaffham Prior came to have such an extravagance but often rivalry between local manors or families caused each to build their own church. One local story is that two sisters had agreed to build one new church and then quarrelled over some of the details, so that in the end they each built the church they wanted. How they divided the congregation of such a small community I don't know. Today only one of the buildings is used for services so the only competition is now between this village and its neighbour—Swaffham Bulbeck.

"*The Fields of Paradise*"

The reason for visiting the churches at Swaffham Prior was to find the grave of the poet and scholar Edwin Muir. I found it eventually by going through the old churchyard, crossing a right-of-way to some new houses, opening a gate in a lane and entering the present burial ground between the original churchyard and a new by-pass.

Because the village is on a chalk ridge above the black fen one feels as if this cemetery is on the side of a hill and, in looking for the grave of an Orkney man, I found myself caught between two ideas of landscape.

The day that had started brightly with generous areas of blue sky and only a few white clouds had now grown much cooler and overcast. The clouds darkened and a cold wind blew over the ridge that put the season back at least a month. Suddenly the cemetery felt bleak and exposed, as if it belonged to a distant and no longer inhabited island.

By the time I found the grave the grey clouds were low on the land and blew in squally showers across the fields. I buttoned my jacket as I walked along the path. It was not ordinary rain, not the kind of rain we are used to in the fens. This was more like a sea-spray or a wet clinging mist blown down from the mountains or coastal rocks. It was a rain born of northern stones rather than of Cambridgeshire soil.

The tall, plain, black headstone also looked different, as if it did not truly belong to these lowlands but to the distant isle of Orkney from which this poet had come. I realized then how right it should be so; for in a very real way the stone's character united the two different landscapes, and I believed that the rain itself had been carried down in the wind from Kirkwall. Perhaps there was a quality in both landscapes that gave them something in common, a rawness and stubbornness that gave them some affinity. Certainly I felt them coming close together in the memory of this one man.

For a second or two my mind went back to the day when I had visited another poet's grave on a hillside, that of Dylan Thomas in Laugharne churchyard. His grave, like this of Edwin Muir, is simple and unpretentious but once spotted is so obviously the grave of the poet you are looking for that you hurry over the grass to get there.

The fine rain sweeping across the ground had brushed the grass in one direction, making it silver with fresh moisture. I knelt down to read the inscription but for a moment it was difficult to see the fine lettering on the dull slab. The clouds had dimmed the sky and the clinging rain on the dust blurred the outlines of the words. But when I rubbed my hand over the face of the stone the surface suddenly shone with the wet and from its newness the simple inscription revealed itself:

In Loving Memory

EDWIN MUIR
Poet

his unblinded eyes
saw far and near the
fields of paradise

born
Orkney, 15th May, 1887.
died
Cambridge, 3rd Jan, 1959.

The words had so much meaning then as I thought again of this poet's own solitary landscape in the Orkneys, of the fields and farms he knew as a child and had described so vividly in his *Autobiography*. I tried to compare them with the black, reclaimed fields he must often have looked at in his last years living in Cambridgeshire. How much was he able to accept this landscape? How often did he long again for the farms and the sea he'd known as a boy? I thought of some of the lines that Edwin Muir had written about that native land when he had been forced to live away from it, when he had been deprived, not only of its inspiration but also of its security:

I take my journey back to see my kindred,
Old founts dried up whose rivers run far on
Through you and me . . .

Through countless wanderings,
Hastenings, lingerings,
From far I come,
And pass from place to place
In a sleep-wandering pace
To seek my home . . .

One foot in Eden still I stand
And look across the other land.
The world's great day is growing late,
Yet strange these fields that we have planted
So long with crops of love and hate.
Time's handiworks by time are haunted,
And nothing now can separate
The corn and tares compactly grown . . .

I stood at the grave for a long time. The rain ceased but I could feel my clothes had become very wet and the ink in which I had copied the inscription on the back of an envelope was now partly washed away. There were no flowers on the grave, only an empty jam-jar and the long grass. The words were the flowers. The words he left in more than two hundred poems, several volumes of prose works, translations, essays, lectures and the autobiography. His wife, Willa, who died in 1970, is now buried with him, her own story told in her book *Belonging*.

Before I left the churchyard a local man had come up to me, and asked if I was 'looking for anyone special'. When I told him about my pilgrimage to Edwin Muir's grave, and who he was, he said, 'Well, you've taught me something I didn't know . . . I didn't realize we 'ad anybody famous buried here. . . . It's a pity its raining 'cus on a clear day you can see Newmarket Racecourse from here. . . .'

Walking back to the church gate I looked over to Priory Cottage, where the Muirs had lived, and where many distinguished writers and scholars had gathered for evenings of readings and conversation, evenings that gave Edwin Muir so much pleasure in the last three years spent away from his own landscape, three years lived quietly and unpretentiously in a village that hardly knew he was there.

The villages of Swaffham Prior and Swaffham Bulbeck are on that unusual ridge of land between what is known as the black fens and the white fens, and driving between the two it is easy to see why. The soil of the higher ground is almost chalky compared with that black land towards Upware. Swaffham Bulbeck looked attractive even on this cool grey day and its history is as interesting as that of Reach. I had lunch at the Black Horse and then took the Stow-cum-Quy road, passing Anglesey Abbey on the way to Cambridge.

The history of Anglesey Abbey is more interesting than its present existence, though for anyone enthusiastic about stately homes and decorative gardens it is a place worth visiting. The original abbey was founded in the reign of Henry I for canons of the Augustan Order. Like most abbeys and monasteries it suffered at the time of the Dissolution and much of the original building ended in ruins. The remains were purchased by the Fokes family towards the end of the sixteenth century and they created the Elizabethan manor that can be seen today. Later owners were to improve the house and gardens and then, in 1926, the manor was bought by Lord Fairhaven and his brother the Honourable Henry Broughton and they extended the garden, lawns and woodlands in an imaginative programme that established Anglesey Abbey again as one of the most popular show-places in East Anglia.

When I left Cambridge later that evening to return home the western sky was clearing. Clouds directed the sun's rays in two broad shafts giving the impression that giant compasses were remeasuring the earth's surface. Drains and dykes were latitudes and longitudes on an enormous chart. Hedgerows and trees were no more than pencil-marks, farms were small dots between distances.

I was undecided which road to take. It had been a long day and there was the temptation to get on to the A1 as quickly as possible to have the advantage of a fast, straight drive home. But that would have meant seeing very little of the evening and would have even added to the strain of travelling, so I was left with roads that went either to Ely, or Cottenham, or ones that left the Huntingdon road to wind through several villages on the way to St Ives and Ramsey.

It had been a few months since I'd last seen Hemingford Abbots and Hemingford Grey so I made a worthwhile detour before continuing to St Ives. With all the commercial traffic of the day gone, the town was very quiet and lovely in the deepening light of the evening. The water of the Ouse flowed slowly under the fifteenth-century bridge with its medieval chapel. The market place was deserted by all but the statue of Oliver Cromwell, a statue rejected by Huntingdon. St Ives market has a long and unbroken tradition going back for nearly nine hundred years and it is still a lively and exciting place to be, especially during a Bank Holiday weekend.

From St Ives to Pidley, Fenton and Warboys the road climbs slowly until for a mile or two you are on the ledge of high ground that offers one of the most dramatic views of the fens. The great plain below was already in shadow by the time I reached Pidley, but my mind went back to occasions when I had been forced to stop the car and look again at the spectacular sight. I thought especially of a late journey I had taken over this road earlier in the year when a lot of the land was under water and there was a full moon in the sky. In the far distance the tiny lights of villages flickered as if they were no more than small boats out at sea. The land itself looked more like an ocean. The light of the moon on the water and the darkness of the night all round made it a chilling and unforgettable experience and it was difficult to keep my eyes on the road as I continued that journey home.

From Warboys to Ramsey the road slowly levels out until you are back on the familiar, flat roads that lead to Whittlesey and Peterborough. The sun was now on the horizon and the clouds reflected briefly the deep shades of red, their bulky, grey masses fringed with fire.

Sunday Mornings

There are times when I think that cities exist just for Sunday mornings, for newspaper sellers and men with nothing else to do but to walk down to town for their Sunday papers.

Other things happen of course. Church-bells ring. People go to church. Travellers pass through the city. But the shops themselves, the banks and offices, are closed and the streets empty after the crowds of Saturday.

I enjoy my walks through these streets to the market place and to the man who occupies the corner doorway of a shop, his newspapers displayed on the floor, his change loose on the ground, his feet in a pool of cigarette ends. You can see so much of the city when it's not working. The roads look wider, the shop-fronts look less commercialized, the usually forgotten corners during the week take on a significance again— old shops not yet demolished, still with living quarters above them and bright window-boxes of flowers; an almond tree in blossom between two building sites; the memory of a certain face looking out from one of the rooms of the now abandoned almshouses; odd traces and reminders of shops and family businesses that have disappeared.

I walk towards the town bridge that crosses the Nene. The stonework of the Customs House is bright and ripples with the reflection from the water. Men walk along the embankment with their dogs. Boys guide their canoes among the swans. The railway lines are empty.

Many of the old shops that I knew when I first started work in the city have made way for car-parks or supermarkets, but there is still one left standing where a printer used to work with the passion and perfection of a true craftsman. At first he used to frighten me with his bluntness. He did not like wasting words nor tolerate fools too charitably. If you wanted a job doing he expected you to know *what* you wanted doing. The copy that was being submitted would be scrutinized for bad syntax, tautology and style. English was not, in fact, his first language but he knew far more about it than many of his customers. I grew to like both his methods and his character. At the time when I was working for the Local Education Authority we often needed printing jobs done in a hurry and I was frequently greeted by the stern words: 'So, it is you, and when do you want this finished? Yesterday, I suppose!' It became a standard phrase between us and I could usually 'phone him in the morning about a rush-job and have the finished work back by half-past four in the afternoon.

One of the last jobs he did before retiring was to print the invitation cards for my mother and father's, and aunt and uncle's, double Golden Wedding Anniversary. When I explained to him what a Golden Wedding was he said, 'You mean the same two people have been married to each other for fifty years, twice in the same family? But that makes one hundred years of marriage! And I thought miracles didn't happen anymore. . . . Who'd *want* to be married to the same person, anyway, for *fifty* years?'

I walk back along the street to the centre of the city. Old men are sitting now in Cathedral Square, enjoying the spring sunshine. A tired waiter looks out from the Chinese restaurant. The bells of St John's church suddenly become silent. The traffic-lights keep changing from red to green, sometimes all to no purpose. There is not much traffic about and this automatic controlling of travellers who are not there has an eerie feel about it. Would the lights go on saying "Stop! Go! Stop! Go!" even if there were no cars at all and the streets permanently empty? Will the traffic lights even outlive us, obediently flashing their signals until their own heart-beats stop?

I pass a cinema where the man is changing the titles for next week's films. At the moment he has one of the letters upside-down. But it is, after all, still only early Sunday morning; perhaps it has been done on purpose, to make people take notice, like the shop-keeper who put a sign in his window on which he had deliberately misspelt a word and his trade doubled that week because of the people who went in just to tell him about his mistake.

There is one small café open for people who, strangely, need somewhere to sit on a bright morning like this to brood their time away over in-different coffee or lukewarm beans-on-toast. There is a stale malingering smell of all yesterday's meals still hanging about the door and a sadness in the eyes that stare back from the windows as I pass.

Although so few people are about on Sunday mornings they all appear to be strangers; strangers and "loners" with nowhere to go and nothing to do, except to buy a paper, light another cigarette, sit and talk to their shadows or walk up and down. It's the most empty morning of the week and, in many ways, the most civilized. Today you don't have to hurry or gamble your life away to cross the roads. The town is yours for the enjoying.

For the newspaper-seller at the corner of the street the day is nearly over. He tells me he has been there since six o'clock in the morning and I find it difficult to believe there's anyone about then to buy papers. But he says, 'You'd be surprised, there's always someone passing by or going home from working all night . . . and by the time you've met the paper train in there's not much point in going home . . . besides, I have to get my stall set out.' I looked at the papers arranged on the floor and could see now that he had put them in some order of popularity.

I walk towards home, along tree-lined roads and then through streets of terraced houses that will soon be pulled down to make way for new terraces. The milkman has just finished his round. Someone is washing his car. Some of the houses have already surrendered to the demolition men and look derelict. Others bravely defy the inevitable and wear bright curtains at clean windows. Some even have gardens that have been planted for yet one more spring.

An old woman appears at one of the doors to take in her milk. I have seen her before, untidy, wizened, furtive and with big eyes of fear, she only squeezes out of the door and reaches for the milk-bottle before dis-appearing again into the haunted shadows of her room. But today she did not disappear quite so quickly. Something caught her attention or stirred the dust of her memory. For a moment she waited and looked up:

> Three days a week she comes to her front door—
> her face as interesting as an old newspaper,
> her body like an apron hung for years in cupboards
> where once she stored her hyacinths for spring.
>
> It's always a brief appearance, just time enough
> to stoop and take her milk from off the step,

and then she disappears again into a room
of shadows, ornaments and plastic flowers.

And yet today she hesitated for a while
as birds bid for their mates and trees lit leaves;
not long, just time enough to wound her winter eyes
and shake the soil of her long-withered roots.

For the rest of the day I sit in the garden, thinking about the faces I have seen in the streets, especially of the old woman who came to her front door and looked up for a moment to appreciate the bright day, the colour of the new leaves against the blue of the sky. As I look up into that blueness again I see that the martins and swallows are back weaving their patterns of flight over our roof-tops, building their nests on to familiar walls. Earth's many wheels, the big and small, are working within each other and never stopping. The pattern has come full circle again. Once more we are at the beginning of roads rather than the ends, or perhaps the end and the beginning are one. The year ahead allows us to believe that twelve months hence is a very long time and the slow dance of light will never tire. The trees sway with a movement that denies they have ever known barrenness. The birds hover with a grace that has never been disturbed by storm. Flowers have changed the garden into a hammock of colour in which I swing and feel the joy of their existence. Why, out of the same dry bulbs or grains of seed, do the same shapes, shades, scents and patterns appear every year? What makes a geranium or a tulip so sure that it will be red or yellow, so consistently and faultlessly year after year?

Tomorrow is now always a day that I feel excited about. I look forward to the morning as something that is waiting to extend this sense of renewal. To sleep is to miss something that might be going on even in the night. To be awake is to be part of an enormous energy and rhythm drawing you into its endless movement.

Light and Skylarks

Just look! I keep telling myself. Just look at that light on the land this morning. Not only on the land but in the air, on buildings, on trees, new leaves, rivers and birds' wings. . . .

The sky vibrates with light. The breeze that passes is so shining it can almost be seen. It is as silvery as pure water released from a newly-dug well. There is not even the smallest feather of a cloud in the sky. It is blue, blue, blue, from every curve and corner of heaven. Just how can I make this light come alive on the page, I ask? How do I convey this excitement to anyone else?

I don't even feel guilty about repeating myself. I have to say it over and over again to make sure it is there, that I am not dreaming. I close my eyes, count up to ten in the mind's dark, then open my eyes again to see what pours into my sight. It is the light. The dazzling brightness of this day when every shoot and blade of grass, when every farm and channel of water is unearthly perfect. And of all my senses I am most grateful to have sight.

But why "unearthly perfect" I ask? Why shouldn't the earth be this beautiful? After all, it's all we know. And why shouldn't the fens have such a morning? Indeed, where else would the light have this quality?

We take so much for granted that it takes a day right out of the ordinary to make us realize what a rich and fruitful planet it is on which we live. We see it every day, our eyes record every minute and we hardly notice it at all. But think what we would say and feel if we were visitors for just *one* day and arrived to find the earth looking like this! We would, I think, be amazed at its beauty, at all its provisions, at its lands and seas, its woods and hills, at all the fields, flowers, crops, birds and animals, at its warmth and light, at the air and space, the sound and colour. We would stand in awe at its abundance. We would be intrigued by the earth's journey round the sun and the subtle changes that came over the land. But the surprise, the revelation would be quite overwhelming if we could only see it for one day. . . . And I appreciate that there would also be the other half of the world we cannot see ourselves, where the earth's abundance has not reached or has been abused, where the wonders of nature are of little significance if that part of earth can offer no more than drought and starvation. I think we take so much for granted, we do moan and grumble without realizing how fortunate we are. What we make, or have failed to make, of our blessings is our responsibility. In one day our mistakes may not appear too obvious or serious. A history of many days takes some of the contentment out of what might otherwise be a perfect morning.

For me today's chief joy, apart from the light and the smell of grass and the flow of water and several other distractions, is the sound of larks. The sky is full of them. They spring up from all parts of the land. They spill out their frenzied arpeggios with such urgency, an eisteddfod of birds, the oldest song-competition in the world. No wonder Tennyson wrote:

> The Lark could scarce get out his notes for joy
> But shook his song together . . .

To sit at a field's edge on a spring day and be so entertained is still one of the great pleasures of being alive. I can remember being excited by the larks' urgent singing from when I was quite a small child and was taken into the fen countryside by my mother. After spending weeks in bed during the winter with asthma or pneumonia it was a sound I looked forward to as much as the sun's warmth. I grew to know in which fields I could expect to find them. I learned that the pitch of their song changed as the days changed. I was puzzled as to why they always sang into the wind. I would stand watching them climb nearer to the sun until my neck ached and they were lost to sight. The passion has not lessened over the years. It is still a sound that takes my mind back to those pre-war years when we also looked for moorhens' nests and watched boys catching eels. I have watched larks as early as January chasing and courting, chattering and competing, trying their wings for the heights that were yet to be achieved. I have counted as many as twenty-three rising from the same field, an exultation in the truest sense. Once I crept very close to a lark perched on a clod of earth and noticed that it had quite long claws. As it would hardly need these for perching on the branches of trees I asked an old man why he thought their claws were so long. He said it was so that they could carry their eggs to safety which, having been laid on the ground, were often in danger of being trodden on by men or horses when ploughing. As soon as that moment of danger arrived the larks simply lifted the eggs from their rough nests and carried them to a safer place. Cattle, he said, never disturbed a nest and always grazed round it. I've never seen this happen so I don't know if the explanation is true or not.

As the heron is, for me, the one essential bird for our waterways, so the larks are the essential song-makers and tenants of our skies. They will be prolific in numbers and notes for the next few weeks. The whole of our countryside would be as impoverished by the loss of birdsong as it would be by the loss of wildflowers. Certainly this landscape would have a terrible emptiness in spring without the lark who rises early in all weathers and scatters his rich crumbs on to our morning table. No wonder Tennyson and Shelley, Shakespeare and Dryden, Wordsworth and Clare, Gerard Manley Hopkins, Edmund Blunden and C. Day Lewis have all written poems about this bird who pours out its full heart "In profuse strains of unpremeditated art", "his rubbed and round pebbles of sound in air's still lake".

And yet it is amazing that the bird has survived at all, for at one time it was hunted and snared and caught in great numbers to sell in London. Fifty years ago men made quite a lot of pocket-money out of netting larks—in some parts of the fens they called it "hingling" and in other parts "trannelling". Larks were considered a delicacy in some well-known restaurants and I was talking to a man in Chatteris only last year who can remember snaring one hundred and fifty birds in one day, and selling them for ninepence a score in 1920. When I asked him if he would do it again he said, 'Ah, if I were 'ard-up.'

The larks that sing above the North Bank of the Nene are as sweet as any and today they have kept up a continuous performance of extravagant coloratura. I walk by the water's edge picking up pieces of wood that have floated downstream, stopping to look at a cluster of riverside flowers, gazing over the washlands towards my home town and the prominent spire of St Mary's church, and all the time the larks keep singing. Just listen! I keep telling myself. Just listen to that incredible sound over the land this morning—and I am grateful too for the sense of hearing. Risking the mantle of Job again, I can't help asking how long will it last. I don't mean my hearing, but the freedom and wildness of this landscape so near to a city.

Threats

Such a question is provoked by realizing what a difference a year makes. We can no longer think in terms of centuries or decades, for even a year can surprise us by the changes it has seen; even a few months can surprise us at how quickly the demands of our times force their presence upon us.

I have been shaken by the rapid encroachment that a developing city has made into the surrounding countryside that we thought would remain unchanged for quite a few years. The solitary landscape, I fear, is being pushed more and more towards extinction, like the wildflower that is hard to find.

This is not meant to sound melodramatic. It is true, and we need to get the demands and the overall cost clearly into perspective. It's not just a question of spending millions of pounds, or knocking down old houses that may not be particularly attractive anyway. It is a question more of destroying the balance and security that the countryside represents.

Within the year that this journal has been in the making, I have seen narrow roads become trunk roads, with shrub-planted roundabouts, lay-bys, traffic-lights and dual-carriageways. Hundreds of old trees have disappeared and miles of ancient hedgerows have been torn out to make way for new housing estates, shopping centres, factories and petrol stations.

A realist will say, 'But all these changes are necessary. You can't be sentimental or selfish over a few fields when hundreds of people need homes and work.' But the demands of the city are unending: they grow and sprawl, plunder and spill over into a countryside that is limited, in the end, by the natural boundaries—the sea.

We are still taking on average 40,000 acres of farmland each year for building purposes—most of it in East Anglia, where the population growth is now above the national level. By the year 2000 it is likely that the fens and quiet corners of Norfolk will have to make room for the expansion of towns that would equal the size of two new cities as big as Norwich. We would need to reclaim the whole of the Wash to compensate for the loss.

To get to and from the cities we have to have new roads, new drains, sewers, electricity, gas, transport and all the other bits and pieces that are necessary to modern life and communication. Cities multiply. Traffic multiplies. People escape from the heartlessness and concrete of a modern city to find something more natural, more human. But so often they take their demands with them, and civilization spreads over every wild tract of heath, and into every lane, until we meet ourselves coming back. The time comes when we can no longer escape, because that from which we long to escape is already there waiting for us. We take it with us, like the tortoise does his shell. We have alienated ourselves from the real elements and protect ourselves with substitutes.

It is, I suppose, a hopeless dilemma in which we find ourselves caught. We want the good things that an affluent and modern society can offer. We also want a place to which we can escape when those things fail, a place in which we can feel free of all the bureaucracy and pressures of modern living. We know that some wildness must be spared if we are to have a refuge; that our land, our countryside, the sea and even the sky, must be protected unless we want to divorce ourselves for ever from the earth and the world of nature. Perhaps that may be the final stage of our evolution, that we at last shake off for all time this feeling of belonging to nature, of belonging to a place.

Usually, though, Man makes the habit of learning too late what it is he really wants. We become military to preserve peace. We have wars to prove to ourselves the ultimate futility of wars. We appear to find satisfaction in repeating our own history. We may learn too late that we cannot repeat the correction, that we cannot take everything for granted and suck the earth dry when the earth is all we have left. It is one thing having a well-organized and scientifically controlled society but it only needs one section of that society to gum up the works and we're back to the dark ages. As the American archaeologist said earlier in the year, 'It's how quickly some things go that worries me.' And perhaps that is the crux of the problems and fears of so many people today. In our own haste and urgency to survive we may not think enough about those who are to come after, a new generation who might like to have had a little of what we are destroying.

Continuing in gloomy mood; perhaps, in the end, we shall have no say in the matter and the earth will be so different that all our values will be questioned. Whether the threatened coming of a new ice-age, starvation, flood, or some other calamity releases us all from responsibility, the future may have little time to be concerned about who is to blame. But calamities, fortunately, do not always happen and forecasts are not always true. Perhaps we shall go on for another thousand years. So what precautions ought we to take? What do we do about being left in charge of preserving this earth? Perhaps one day we shall have found the answers and will have come to terms with our demands and what the earth can give.

The great value of a spring day is that it always gives this hope. The year begins again for the ten thousandth time with all its rituals, promises, expectations, dreams and good intentions. The plough turning over the soil, the drill planting the seed, the sun warming those crops that are already growing, the long days and the extensive light all belong to a new genesis. And so does Man.

The clouds that drift across today's sky are new-made clouds that have never travelled the sky before. The water in the rivers and dykes is no longer stale, stagnant or tired but comes fresh from the spring's beginning and melted snows. Everything is being given a second chance and there is great excitement in being out in the fresh, timeless air on a day that says, 'All this survives in you, in the individual, in that infinitesimal unit which may only be human but which has the power to choose.'

Reassurances

Today I realize, I think for the first time, that it is not just the quality of light that is so distinctive but the variety of light that exists at the same moment.

To the east the light is brown and golden as the clouds and sun mix in vivid swirling contrasts; to the south it is a calm silvery-green without any movement and to the west it is cornflower-blue and white; while in the north the shades darken to battleship grey as storm clouds gather in convoys over the Lincolnshire fens.

If I were to take a colour photograph in each direction, it would be very difficult to convince a stranger that the four pictures were taken on the same day and at the same moment, for the contrasts are like four seasons having a reunion. The space above me and around me is vast enough to present four skyscapes in one, that contradict and complement each other, creating an enormous crystal ball of many images and wonders.

This variety of sky seems to dwarf the earth even more today. Church spires and brickyard chimneys are no more than headless stalks of flowers or reeds standing in a marsh of light. Looking from the sky to the fields a few cattle appear no bigger than ladybirds, and sheep look like shy wind-flowers.

Only when I reach the streets of the town do I feel that people and buildings are becoming normal again, regaining their true stature in proportion to the size of the houses and shops.

I stand for a while under the four-hundred-year-old Buttercross on Whittlesey market square, where produce has been bartered and sold, where men have been hired or sacked, where revivalist preachers and politicians have ranted with varying degrees of eloquence and conviction. I always enjoyed a good orator, whatever his doctrine, and can remember some of the speakers who held us spell-bound forty years ago. As a child nothing gave me goose-pimples quicker than a fiery speech or sermon. I responded to words then, never dreaming that one day I would choose to use them for my own ideas, whimpers or rantings. A good orator and a man with the gift of the gab still appeals to me as much as any other sensation, making the blood thump in the head, until I feel myself an easy victim of any hysteria. The power of language to console, as well as provoke, is as dramatic as a full orchestra.

But today there are no soap-boxes, tub-thumpers, preachers, fanatics, goose-pimples or hair-raising. The town goes on quietly with its business. The war memorial with St George and the Dragon is still there with its lists of the town's dead. The Post Office and the George Hotel have survived many of the changes. St Mary's church is only a tombstone's throw away and, for a man I start talking to, the memories are as fresh as ever—Hospital Sundays, Plough-Witch-Mondays, Straw-Bear Tuesdays, jubilees and riots, feasts and Sunday School outings and many more events, big and small, important and lost.

I asked him about the Sunday School outings for I had seen photographs of some of the gatherings of fifty and sixty years ago.

'Well, for a lot on us in them days,' he said, 'that was the only chance you got of an 'oliday . . . just one day and usually at Hunstanton.'

'All the Sunday Schools went on the same day, didn't they?'

'Most of 'em did, I think. I know there used to be a rare ole crowd on us then, as many as three hundred, all with buckets and spades and bags of sandwiches. . . . There were quite a lot of chapels in town then and on the day we met for the outing the town band used to play us all down to the station just as if we were going off to war, which weren't far wrong sometimes. When things didn't allus sort themselves out prop'ly there could be a few upsets. . . . I reckon more young Christian blood was spilt on that day than was shed in the Civil War.'

'As bad as that?'

'Well, nearly. I've come to the conclusion that belonging to a place of worship don't make you any better or worse than anybody else when it's everybody for himself, and I can certainly remember we 'ad a few good scraps afore the band even struck up and got us on our way. . . . I couldn't go myself one year 'cus I got my eye split open with a clout from a bucket.'

'What do you think of the town now?'

'It's all right in a way, I suppose, but you don't know everybody any more and I don't care all that much for the noise. There's still a few of us old 'uns left but all we can do is mooch about looking for someone to talk to and when we do we only talk about the past. . . . Everybody has to make what they can of their own times, don't they? I don't envy the youngsters today but they're better off 'n what we were.'

The stone pillars of the old Buttercross were warm with the sunlight and the stories they had heard so many times before. I walked away from the market square (which older residents still call "the hill") and sauntered along familiar streets with my own more recent memories. I passed the

M

schools I'd attended and spoke to one or two people who'd gone to those schools with me, and even met a woman who taught me during the war years. We knew each other now well enough to laugh about some of the inadequacies and lessons we had then in crowded classrooms, heated by ancient and reluctant tortoise stoves, on which buckets of water steamed to sweeten the air. She had taught my brothers and had spent more than one extra half-hour on Friday afternoons encouraging me to read.

It's a safe feeling, a secure feeling; where one half expects to see faces that one knows are no longer alive but, because of their presence once, give some kind of assurance, a harbour of contentment even when the quayside is crumbling and the boats not very seaworthy. I never cease to be surprised at the pride some of these people have in belonging to a place, and more than once, when I have been relating an amusing anecdote to someone they've said something like, "Oh, he was my uncle", or "She was my sister-in-law"—so a lot of very good stories have to be kept to oneself; they may have to wait generations before they can appear in print. The relatives do not mind the stories being known, provided they are kept secret.

Almost a Postscript

During the writing of this journal, I have been fortunate to meet and talk with a number of people who, in their own quiet and unpretentious way, have been preserving their own records of life in the fens. Most of them have a long history of belonging to this part of East Anglia. Some have been able to establish that they are direct descendants of early English families, and others know now that their ancestors came over with the French Huguenots more than three hundred years ago, or have Scottish blood in their veins from those Scottish prisoners-of-war who stayed behind after helping Vermuyden with his drainage works.

I have sat and talked with these people in small cottages, manor houses, council flats, high-ceilinged rooms of old houses, village pubs and libraries. Many of them were strangers before I was introduced to them, or found them by accident. And, fortunately, accidents have a convenient way of happening at the right time. Chance remarks made in the most unlikely places suddenly lead to contacts with families who have been doing their own detective work, families with rooms full of rare books, or modest possessions, they have preserved for five generations; octogenarians with remarkably good memories who quite casually produce an article that belonged to Samuel Pepys, or the skates that belonged to "Turkey" Smart.

One evening I found myself talking to a relative of that great skating family, the Smarts, and a week later in a stationer's shop I found myself talking to the brother of the Mrs Harris I've written about in an earlier chapter, and he told me about Turkey Smart's skates. He did not know who I was or that I had been talking to his sister. On another occasion I met someone who had some first editions of John Clare's poetry, and one day I sat with a man who, having fought in the Boer War, returned to his village and has never left it again in all these years. Why? Because he said when he came home he wanted to stay home and keep racing pigeons. 'I let them do my travelling now,' he said. 'I think you're a happier man if you can find all you want out of life in your own town. . . . I was born here and I may as well die here.'

At one ancient house in the Fens, that has a thirteenth-century arch in one of its walls, I had been invited to see some old photographs, but ended up holding priceless books, including an early Prayer Book, with wooden covers, a Breeches Bible, beautifully engraved atlases, old paintings (some on wood and found under floor-boards), and a pictorial record of life in that village for many years. None of these treasures had been deliberately collected or hoarded, they had been handed down through the generations of local families who had taken some pride in their achievements, their early ancestors frequently among the tenants or farmers who rented the land reclaimed by the Duke of Bedford's Gentlemen Adventurers in the seventeenth century.

Some of these people, understandably, do not want to be identified in this story, nor do they wish their possessions to be too widely publicized. I can only record my gratitude in being allowed into their homes, to search through their private papers and, for a few hours, to have been part of their lives.

All these occasions and meetings have gone a long way in my own search towards a deeper understanding of this solitary landscape, *my* landscape—although I realize now how selfish and possessive one can be about one's own backyard. As one old fenman said to another who'd been bragging about his family's connections with a certain village for nearly three hundred years, 'Why, bor! yew're nothin' but a newcomer, my family 'ev bin 'ere for four hundred years, that they 'ev.'

So, whether I remember the evenings I spent in long talks with people like Mrs Gill, with Hugh Douglas or Mrs Harris, or with Hugh and Renate Cave, as well as the many other friends I have made this year, I am sure of one thing, that even if we do prefer a certain landscape and like to think of it as all ours there are many other individuals with a similar feeling for the place, who have set out on their own discoveries and with as much love. Certainly I found there are a lot of people in the fens whose claims for this countryside can equal my own.

But in remembering all these conversations the question returns again and again—"who are we?" Looking back through what is, after all, only a brief history, the mind asks, "From which land or tribe have we come on our journeys? Into which dark shadow do we hope to feel the sun finally penetrate? Why do we feel we belong to a special place? Are we, in some strange way, grateful for the invisible chains that hold us, or do we hope that one day the chains will be broken, if they have not been already?"

Who began it? Who played the dark music
one night under the stars and mixed the seeds
in the veins of this soil making a chain
for the child's neck, a legendary thread
to guide him back to his unbroken dream?

Who fixed the pattern of our steps on roads
that led to everywhere but home until
the blood heard names giving identity
to forms and places only whispered in
the confidence of sleep, the ancient dance?

Who are we when the pedigrees are told
and each compelling spirit brought to earth
where we, as strangers, learn to recognize
the face of someone who was someone's son
before the music of the first dark stranger's birth.

I think of that old man who gave my father life
and from his homespun wisdom and bright eyes
taught me to trace the footprints on a path
that went through fields and water, grass and skies
until I felt his strong blood in my stride.

It's true, there is a place to which we turn
whether before or after death comes down
and leaves this solitary landscape dumb.
My luck was finding in these childless veins
the seeds that danced one night and closed this chain.

A Returning

I have been kept away from seeing and writing about this landscape for nearly three weeks and now I am back I find myself asking still more questions about it to which I can find no answers.

The fields look very alive again, and, in some areas, quite active. So is this really a solitary landscape after all, or is that the way I like to see it? Is it because I am mostly alone when I sit or stand, walk or drive into its immense regions? Do I find, or take with me, the mood and character I hope will be there? Am I trying to understand the landscape, or myself?

What would this landscape be like anyway, without our eyes to see and our minds to interpret? What makes the solitariness, the timelessness, the wildness, or fulfils the hunger?

I have returned to it again and know that all the feelings I have tried to express are still there in me; but what of the earth? Does it respond? How much does it know?

This morning I saw a stoat run swiftly across the road and the light of the sun caught its sandy-coloured pelt, so that for a split second there was a moment of glory. And surely that would have been there whether I had seen it or not. The flash of iridescence on the wing of a kingfisher or the brief beauty of light on the bark of a tree are not works of the imagination. They are there. They exist. They would happen without us. We are the lucky ones who see.

There is the stillness and the movement, the rhythm and the silence. The sun has no glory without the movement of the earth. The wind has no meaning without the weight of a cloud or the resistance of a tree. The silence is nothing without the soul's power to feel silence. So, in the end, we are all elements that are interwoven, related to, dependent on and of value to each other. We and the earth, the grass and the skies, the light and the sea, are one. But does this mean that the earth of which I have been writing ceases to exist if we are no longer part? Is this fen country capable of existing without my response to it, without my presentation of it as the solitary landscape?

For as long as man remains I must believe that this land will continue with its seasons, sunsets, storms, heat-waves, snows, mists and rainfalls. It may even continue with its harvests and crops, with its labourers and farmers, its houses and cities. But what will happen after we have become the dust on the wind, or the white bone in the soil, when we have become even less than the bog-oaks? Will others come and find in this special landscape a similar challenge, a similar joy and the same satisfaction?

In the end, I suppose, it is always a very private affair we have with the earth and sky, the winter and spring. We may share many moments of pleasure and exploration with others, but perhaps the discoveries are personal and secret, even if we find any answers at all, and even if we spend a long time putting the ideas down on paper.

I believe the earth feels and knows of our feelings. This landscape is un-compromising and aloof. It will not be flattered or tempted by cheap morsels for the sake of curiosity or an instant camera-shot. I have learned how demanding it can be. It is a god that expects devotion but does not always thank you for it. We may have shaped and fashioned this land. We may have made it what it is for our own purposes. But the ancient spirit, that breathes in every acre of soil or vein of water, is what will survive. It is the spirit of the land that demands such allegiance.

That is what matters. That is what we secretly want. We want to belong to the winter and summer, the snowfall and sun, the horizon and sky, the clouds and stars. The untried and the impatient may not understand. To experience the spirit of this landscape is a greater thrill than entering the undiscovered tomb of a great pharaoh. There has to be awe and reverence, humility as well as excitement, for we too are disturbing Time. We too are trying to understand both the past and the present. We are the subjects. We respond. We serve. We take, absorb and try to interpret. The silence sometimes has frightened me. The solitariness has made me tremble. But I have been to that edge where neither land nor sea will give in to each other and have felt the most extraordinary influences of this land. I have grown young and old at the same time. I have been alone and heard the voices of unknown ancestors. I have stood and felt the weight of my body evaporate until my spirit buried itself deep in the earth or wandered into those dark fields of space. I have seen my body walking on distant horizons. I have seen my face stare back at me from the waters.

We can only carry so much around with us in our physical being, but what we really are, or can be, is as limitless as the air and the light of the land I have been writing about. And I would always come back to this land to continue what will always be but a beginning.

Tonight on this quiet riverbank there is now no doubt in my mind. The night and the silence reassure. The ancient blood beats with a steady contented rhythm. Each breath is a mile long and a mile deep.

In the distance the familiar farms are only just visible. To the west the outlines of the city begin to perforate the two shades of growing darkness. To the south the lights of my home town are as constant as they have always been.

Here, in this late and June night stillness, I look over the fields that have chained the years and the people together in a conflict of bondage and freedom, repression and security.

Between here and there are the shadows, summers, winters, songs and features of five generations and ten centuries. The voices and faces stare back at me from the water. Echoes of the dark music and ancient dance stir at the back of my eyes, trying to get out.

The river waits. The grass is preparing for morning. The smoke from the brickyard chimneys smoulders on the sky's hearth. I am absorbed by the approaching mist and silence.

I look towards the road half-hidden beyond the willow trees and think I see the shadow of a man walking towards me. . . .

Without him there would have been nothing.

Index

Compiled by H. E. Crowe